CW00971701

"SACK YOUR BOSS!"

says

Jonathan Jay

Quit your job and turn your passion into your profession!

Crown House Publishing Limited
www.crownhouse.co.uk

First published by

Crown House Publishing Ltd
Crown Buildings, Bancyfelin, Carmarthen, Wales, SA33 5ND, UK
www.crownhouse.co.uk

and

Crown House Publishing Company LLC
4 Berkeley Street, 1st Floor, Norwalk, CT 06850, USA
www.CHPUS.com

British Library of Cataloguing-in-Publication Data
A catalogue entry for this book is available
from the British Library.

10-digit ISBN 1845900022
13-digit ISBN 978-184590002-1

LCCN 2005928405

Printed and bound in the UK by
Creative Print and Design Group

To my parents, Sue and Roland, who turned
their passion into their profession and always supported
me in doing the same. Thank you.

ACKNOWLEDGEMENTS

The Coaching Academy wouldn't exist without its training team, who give up their weekends month after month, and the head office staff, who do all the stuff I hate, and do it all far better than I ever could. I'd also like to thank my bank manager Tony Stanley Jones, for believing in me, and Rob Rendle for persuading me to write this book. Constantly, he challenged me to aim higher and prevented me from making too many mistakes.

CONTENTS

Introduction   **iii**

JOIN THE SACK YOUR BOSS REVOLUTION

1 Do you hate your job enough to sack your boss?   **3**

2 Change your life for ever   **10**
Setting your goals   12
Why sack your boss?   14
Do you have what it takes?   17

3 You've done it! Now what?   **20**

SETTING UP YOUR BUSINESS

4 Self-management   **31**
Action orientation   33
Take responsibility   34
Turn negative into positive   37
Imitate excellence   38
Turn fear into focus   38
Uncover your hidden talents   39
Develop yourself   39
Expect the unexpected   39

5 Finance and accounts   **41**
Cash flow   44
Keeping costs down   54
What price should I charge?   56

6 Professionalism   **61**
Your image and your company's image   61
Business premises   65
What equipment do I need?   66

7 Planning   **67**
Your business plan   67
Five-year plan   71
Time management   72
Working *on* the business, not *in* it   75
Technical stuff   76

RUNNING YOUR BUSINESS

8 A crash course in marketing   **81**
How to find customers   82
1.   Developing your client list   83
2.   Networking   86
3.   Join a professional organisation   91
4.   Public relations   93
5.   Advertising   103
6.   Referrals   107
7.   The Internet   110
8.   Write a newsletter   116
9.   Joint ventures   120
10.   Public speaking   125
11.   Trade shows   129
12.   Leaflets and brochures   131
13.   Write a 'report'   134
14.   Writing a book   138
15.   Promotions and promotional material   140
16.   Niche marketing   142

9 A crash course in selling   **144**
When the phone rings   145
Customer service   150

10 Growing your business   **153**
Keep your hands on the cash   154
Managing people   155
Exit strategy   159

So what are you waiting for?   **161**
Tell me how you sacked your boss   164

Bibliography   **165**

INTRODUCTION

Six years ago, I started my own company with £145. Today, that business, the Coaching Academy, is worth £25 million and has become Europe's largest and most successful training school for coaches.

Coaching is one of the fastest-growing industries in the world. More people than ever are following the trend set by sportsmen and women and hiring a coach. In sport, coaches help athletes reach the top, and they can do the same in business and other areas of people's lives. With the help of a coach we can achieve our dreams and ambitions.

By becoming a business coach, I have already helped more than 5,000 people onto the road of self-employment. I was also a TV presenter on BBC2's highly successful relocation show, Get A New Life, which takes British people and helps them start a new life abroad. Many of those featured started new businesses as well.

According to the British government's own figures, more than half the people working in the UK believe they have the skills to start up a business, but most of them lack the courage to sack their boss and hire themselves. Sacking your boss and setting up on your own is a high-risk venture. Eight out of every ten new businesses fail in the first five years and others fail in the next five, many because their owners have not learned the necessary skills to go it alone. This book contains all the inside information you need to join the revolution and succeed in turning your passion into your profession by sacking your boss.

"JOIN THE SACK YOUR BOSS REVOLUTION"

CHAPTER 1

DO YOU HATE YOUR JOB ENOUGH TO SACK YOUR BOSS?

A quiet revolution is taking place in Britain. Every week nearly three thousand people sack their boss. They have had enough of working for someone else and want to start working for themselves.

The chances are that, if you have picked up this book, you are unhappy working for an employer and are thinking of going it alone. Believe me, you are not the only person who feels this way. A large percentage of people hate their boss and, if they don't hate their boss, they hate their job. Our research has shown that seven out of ten people would quit today if they had a chance and that an astonishing 14 million people in the UK are dissatisfied with their work and would love to give up their job. Most would love the freedom to be able to work *when* they want, *how* they want, *with whom* they want and *wherever* they want, doing something they love, rather than something they loathe.

Do you hate the restrictions your employer puts on your life? Are you doing something or working for someone you do not believe in? Do you get up every morning and battle through rush-hour traffic to do a job that gives you absolutely zero fulfilment for seven and a half hours of your day? If you are one of these people, then you will spend your working time daydreaming about a life in which you can do exactly what you want every day of the year.

In your lifetime, you will spend at least 78,144 hours at work. If you are going to spend that much time at work you should at least enjoy it and, if you are not enjoying what you do at all, you must do something about it before it is too late. If you are unhappy in your job, do something about it right now. You don't have to suffer endless weeks, months and years in a job you dislike just for the pay cheque. Here is something you can try.

Work out your life expectancy, then subtract your age now. Multiply that number by 52. Write down the answer and then put that number of marbles into a glass jar. That is how many weeks you have left to live. Every Saturday, take out a marble. It will demonstrate the harsh reality of actually seeing your life diminish in front of you. It is not pleasant but it does make you realise that time is passing on, whether you like it or not.

 People who feel just like you *are* taking charge of their lives, getting rid of their bosses and working for themselves instead.

You are probably thinking, 'I'd like to sack my boss but I don't dare. It's too risky.' Well, take my word for it: people who feel just like you *are* taking charge of their lives, getting rid of their bosses and working for themselves instead. In 2003 alone, an astonishing 465,000 new businesses started up in the United Kingdom. That means that the equivalent of the entire population, say, of Bradford or nearly the whole county of Cornwall have sacked their bosses and hired themselves. I meet so many people who dream of starting up their own businesses, yet something always holds them back. When I ask them what is preventing them, I get lots of excuses. However, when I investigate a little further, I find out that what is really holding them back is the simple fact that they do not know what to do.

There are hundreds of books about setting up your own business. Most are written by academics, gurus and so-called experts, many of whom have never run their own successful business. Quite a few business start-up books are sponsored by banks and most banks do not know the first thing about running a small business. All they see of your company is your bank statement, and businesses are not just about bank statements. *Sack Your Boss!* is completely different. It is a hands-on, real-life account of how to get from minus on your bank statement to being healthily in the black, with an explanation of the stages in between. It is always better to learn from someone who has done it, rather than someone who is just theorising.

As well as great tips, advice and practical inside information on setting up a business, I will also explain how I did it. Over the last eight years I have started businesses that did not work until I hit on a highly successful formula that turned my business into Europe's largest coach-training school worth £25 million. I will tell you what worked, so you can emulate it. I will also tell you what did not work, so you can avoid it altogether; or, perhaps you will be able to figure out why it went wrong, and then you won't make the same mistake yourself. Some of my advice may be a bit controversial and sometimes I am a little outspoken, but there is not one ounce of theory in this book. It is entirely practical. There is no business-school language here and you certainly don't need a degree to understand it.

 Whatever your background, whatever your age, whatever your education, you can put the tips in this book into practice and sack your boss.

Whatever your background, whatever your age, whatever your education, you can put the tips into practice. I want to inspire you to have belief in yourself and to go out there, sack your boss and make it happen for you.

It does not matter what industry you are going into, whether you are buying and selling or hiring yourself out as a consultant, the advice is easily adaptable to any business. I know that the tricks of the trade that will tend to work in one industry will work in another. Whatever business you are in, you can use, for instance, the advice on:

■ using press releases to get free publicity;

■ discovering ways to get referrals; and

■ the best and cheapest way to land new business, to get you exactly where you want to be.

It is very easy to get stuck in the box of traditional thinking. The secret is to look at what works in other people's businesses and adapt it to your own. The great thing about every piece of practical advice in this book is that you can do it immediately. There is nothing here that takes six months of planning to make it happen. Don't think that starting your own business is the easy option. It is not. You will probably work harder than at any other time in your entire life. What this book will do is give you short cuts to working smarter, not just harder.

If you are one of the 465,000 people thinking about going it alone this year, you need to have a plan of action so that, when the day comes and you do dump your boss, you are not completely on your own. Do not walk out of your job today with nothing else planned, because that would just be foolish and you would end up begging your employer to rehire you, which he or she probably wouldn't do.

I will show you how to sack your boss, hire yourself and remain on good terms with your former employer. In fact, I will demonstrate how he or she can become one of your greatest allies in your new venture.

Sack Your Boss! takes you through all the practical steps you will need on the road to becoming your own boss and making your new company successful. I can show you how to emulate the successful entrepreneurs and to replicate the things they do that will make you succeed.

The one thing you must have in bucketfuls is self-belief. If you do not believe in yourself, no one else will.

When you first learn to drive, you think about every move: mirror, signal, manoeuvre. After a while you stop thinking about it and do it automatically. In the same way you can rewrite your 'mental DNA' so that, after a while, it becomes second nature to follow the successful pattern of operating in business. The one thing you must have in bucketfuls is self-belief. If you do not believe in yourself, no one else will. If you don't know where you are heading, no one is going to follow you. If you are going to be the head of a business, you have to know where it is going. If you do not have self-belief when you get your first knock-back – and there will be many on the road ahead – you will stop and give up. You are allowed to doubt yourself occasionally – but not too much!

Everyone who starts up a new business worries about money and you will be pleased to hear that every piece of advice in this book can be put into operation quickly, easily and for next to no money at all. You don't need your life savings to set up your own business. You can do it on a shoestring. The biggest mistake people make when they start a business is to go out and get a bank loan. They start off their business life in debt. Instead of being accountable only to themselves, they are suddenly accountable to the bank as well.

There are people like the vacuum cleaner tycoon James Dyson, who remortgaged his house because he believed in what he was doing, and the game paid off eventually. He is the exception. For most people, it is a complete and utter disaster. At least if you start off with zero money, you do not start off with negative equity. Also, when you have no money in the bank, you work smarter, and you use your brain, rather than just writing a cheque. I will demonstrate how you can work smartly.

A computer software inventor came to see me a couple of years ago. He had a very good training course on a CD-ROM. He needed money to finish it off and he tried to sell me shares in his company. He needed a huge amount of money to finish his project. I could not see where he was spending the money and it turned out that he needed thirty people to write for the project. I told him to subcontract the work out and get the writers to submit their pieces by the following Friday. They were only doing a few thousand words each, so it was quite feasible. That was two years ago and recently I asked him how it was going. 'Oh, we're nearly there,' he replied. Someone had pumped £200,000 into the project, the money had gone and he reckoned he needed another £200,000 to complete it. Even if he does complete it having spent another £200,000, he will never sell enough CD-ROMs to recoup the money. He has a very good idea but he should not be running the business.

Another important warning is that, when you do sack your boss, do not take on a partner. The reason people take on partners or fellow directors is that they do not believe in the business themselves. It is far easier to go into business with someone else than by yourself because that way you have someone with whom you can share the blame. When you work with someone else the arguments usually boil down to one thing: the division of labour. One person always believes they are working harder than the other. Whether they are or not is not the point. Each *believes* they are working harder and, as a result, most partnerships and business relationships break down.

The entrepreneur never works with anyone else because he or she wants to take all the glory. There is a bit of an ego trip involved because it is all about saying, 'I can do this. I can prove it to you and to myself.' Sharing it with half a dozen people really does not work. So many businesses are set up by people who meet up in a restaurant and say, 'Well, we all bought a quarter of the pizza, so let's each take 25 per cent of the business.'

The one thing I would always advise is never, ever give away bits of your business. The people who want a share have not earned it. They do not deserve it. If you are doing the work, you deserve to own the business. No one will want it when you are not successful, but, once you start making a success of a venture, all sorts of people will want a slice of the action. They will come along and offer their money and expertise, but you should turn it down. It is hard to do but it is the most sensible thing in the long run.

The first part of *Sack Your Boss!* is about how to get yourself on target and how to set your goals for the future. You have to identify where you want to be in your life in a few months, next year and in five years. Just now you might be a bit cynical about setting goals for yourself. You are probably saying, 'I've never planned anything in my life but I'm doing all right.' Check that jar of marbles when you say that. Look how many weeks you have left. In twelve months, your life will have moved on, whether you set yourself goals for the future or not. How much better would it be to go into the next twelve months knowing exactly where you are going? You will need to know how to plan your business and make it work for a five-year period, and, along the way, I will give you practical advice through my own experience. Throughout the book, you will find personal action plans that will help you to make your dream come true.

After helping you to sack your boss and set up your business, this book will reveal the secrets to laying the cornerstone of running any business, which is how to get customers. Without customers you do not have a business. You will then need to keep your customers happy, and satisfied customers will lead you to new clients.

When you start your own company, the only person who can decide which line of business you should go into is you. It has got to be something you have a passion for because that passion will keep you going when everything is going wrong – as, more than likely, it will. You have also got to have a business from which there is some money to be made, otherwise you are going to be worse off than when you were working for someone else. One way to determine whether there is money in that business is to find out if other people are making a profit in the same business. If they are not and you have something that is sufficiently different, then maybe it will work for you. A lot of gut instinct goes into something like this, but there also has to be a lot of common sense.

Traditionally, it makes sense to stay away from a business whose profit margins are so small that you have to sell thousands of units of your product to make any money. Another way to create a good enterprise is to do something that creates high customer satisfaction – in other words, a business that pleases your customers so much they are happy to refer you to others.

You also want a business in which you are not paid weeks or months after the job is completed, because bad cash flow will quickly strangle and kill your venture. Then it has to be something that is going to be fun. A company called Piranha Marketing says that any business should be ELF – Easy, Lucrative and Fun, rather than HALF – Hard, Annoying, Lame and Frustrating! The amazing thing is that, when you are looking for opportunities, they will come to you. You will see them everywhere. When your mind is open to ideas you will be spoiled for choice. You must sift through all these opportunities to find the things that will not only appeal to you but also will work. It took me three years to find the idea that really worked for me. It did not happen overnight and I had read just about every book there was on setting up a business. If I had had a book like this, I would have found my successful formula in half the time because my mistakes and achievements will help you to be successful. Here is where the journey to sacking your boss and hiring your own staff starts.

CHAPTER 2

CHANGE YOUR LIFE FOR EVER

Most people now have an average of seven careers in their working lives – not *job* changes but *career* changes. So if you are unhappy with your lot in life, why not get yourself a new career and, instead of landing yourself a new boss, why not hire yourself? Do you dream of a life where you are in charge?

Thirteen years ago, when I was just nineteen, I picked up a book that changed my life for ever. I read in *Awaken the Giant Within*, by the top motivator Tony Robbins, that it is you who decides your future. If you are not the person you want to be, you can change. It was amazing because, until that point, I'd always thought our lives were preordained. I hadn't realised that I had any control over my future but in fact you really can make your future whatever you want it to be.

Then I read the biography of Richard Branson, founder and chairman of Virgin. At the time, I was working as a stage hypnotist at hotels on Ibiza. In the evening, I worked for two hours, then I would go out drinking in bars. During the day, I would lie on the beach doing absolutely nothing, waiting for those two hours' work for which I would get paid to come around again. It might sound idyllic but I was bored until I started reading about Branson. As I read about his amazing career, first as the boss of Virgin Records and then as the creator of Virgin Atlantic Airways, I thought, 'He's never going to be bored doing all that.' And I realised that what I wanted to be more than anything in the world was an entrepreneur. There and then I cancelled my stage season two months early and returned to Britain. My decision did not go down well with the fourteen hotels I worked for, but I knew I had to do something about my life. I had to take control of my future.

One thread ran through Richard Branson's book, and that was his unshakeable self-belief. He tried so many things that didn't work but he never gave up. Someone who is successful in business must have total self-belief. You have got to believe, even though everyone around you is saying it will never work and telling you to give up. It was at that moment I knew that one day I would be a success. There would be tears and heartache along the way but I just knew that being an entrepreneur would work. People talk a lot about luck. No one ever says it to my face but I know some people say, 'Jonathan was in the right place at the right time. He was lucky. I had an idea like that before he did.' The vital difference is that they didn't do it and I did. There's a big difference between thinking about something and actually taking action.

 There is no doubt in my mind that if you want the life that you dream of, whatever it may be, if you want it badly enough and you are prepared and willing to take action, then there's absolutely no question that you can get it.

I always say that the harder I work the luckier I become. There is no doubt in my mind that, if you want the life you dream of, whatever it may be, if you want it badly enough and are prepared and willing to take action, then there's absolutely no question that you can get it. It doesn't have to involve money or fast cars and living in plush hotels while travelling the world – it can be just a great family life. If one of your goals is to set up on your own, this book will help you on the road to business success.

When you work for yourself you can create the future that *you* want rather than the future that your employer wants, but you need to do it properly. Setting up your own business needs to be done carefully. Many people who sack their boss do it very badly and end up in an even worse situation than before.

They used to hate their boss and now they hate themselves. You can avoid some of the basic mistakes made by many self-employed people.

They get themselves into a situation where they are not equipped with the right skills to run a business. It can all go horribly, horribly wrong. Often a new business gets out of control and ends up with huge debts. I have made a study of why some people make it and others don't. I want to help you make sure that you are armed with all the advice you need to be successful. I'm not rash enough to claim to have all the answers – I don't – but I do know the elements that make it more likely that you will be successful.

SETTING YOUR GOALS

Think of an archer like Robin Hood, who was so good that he could hit the bull's-eye every time. Now place a blindfold over his eyes and turn him around half a dozen times. He will never hit the target now. It is the same with life: if you cannot see the target, how can you hit it?

You have to have a goal to aim for. Too many people wander aimlessly through life with no real idea about what they want to do. That is why you must set goals and give yourself something to aim for. It is a way of taking control of your own life.

Setting goals is no different from being an architect. You are the architect of your life. You would not dream of building a house without architect's drawings. Without a plan, the house would be a disaster, and so it is with your life. What is the plan for your and your family's future? So many people put more thought into planning their annual holidays than they do planning their lives and what they actually want from them. Your goals are what you want from your life. They can be anything at all, for example:

- I want to be chief executive of a company employing 50 people and turning over £20 million a year.

- I have had enough of not having enough money – I want to be financially independent

- I want a better relationship with my children.

- I want more time to play squash.

- I want to leave the office by 6 p.m. every day.

- I've had enough of getting up in the morning and never finding anything to wear.

- I want a walk-in wardrobe.

Perhaps you have just moved into a new neighbourhood and you want to throw a party at your house in four weeks' time, inviting twenty people whom you don't yet know. Your goal could be to find twenty people whom you will get to know well enough to invite round to your house within a month. We all go around with a wish list in our heads, but you must *write down* your goals. It is an amazing fact that, when you write something down, it crystallises your thoughts and dreams. You are not only committing that goal to paper but also committing yourself to that goal.

The first time I set goals for myself was back in 1993. I can look back at them and smile now. Top of my list was to have a mobile phone. Back then cell phones were not as common as they are now, and I really wanted one. I also wanted to have my own car. I wrote all my goals down and, six months later, I put a tick beside every single item on the list. I did it again and I have continued to write down my goals ever since. There is nothing mystical about this process: it is just good, plain common sense.

Most people's level of planning does not extend beyond their shopping list. If you go to the supermarket without a list and you're anything like me, you wander aimlessly up and down the aisles, doubling back on yourself. Finally, you leave the store with a trolley load of things you really did not need. You will also have forgotten the really important things that you went there for in the first place. But, if you make a list at home and take it with you, you will work your way down that list and make your time far more effective. You think to yourself, 'Yeah, I've got everything' – and it makes you feel good. That is what you feel like when you set yourself business goals and achieve them.

 **You should look at your goals on a daily basis. Some people stick them on the bathroom mirror so that the first thing they see in the morning is their objectives.**

You should look at your goals on a daily basis. Some people stick them on the bathroom mirror so that the first thing they see in the morning is their objectives. It is no different from a sales person having targets to meet. Your goals have to be realistic. You can set a target for a sales team but, to work, it has to be achievable. It is the same with your personal goals.

Suppose your goal is to become a millionaire, which is a perfectly good goal over a realistic timescale. You cannot say, 'I want to be a millionaire by next Tuesday evening,' because, short of winning the lottery, it is not going to happen. (By the way, the lottery is the only tax that people pay voluntarily.) So, to be a millionaire, you need to write a list of how much you need to earn over a realistic period. You also need to identify the people or organisations that can help you reach your goal.

I have started doing this only recently, but I now ask people I meet if there is anything I can do to help them achieve their ambitions. The offer is genuine and I am glad to make it. I have learned that if you help other people get what they want, you will get everything in life that you want. So I help other people get what they want by teaching coaching skills. As a result, they help me get what I want in life, which is the successful business I now have, plus a whole lot of fun running it. Setting definable goals is the cornerstone of life as well as your business.

WHY SACK YOUR BOSS?

Millions of people feel they can do better than their boss. Whether they can or not is a different matter. It is irrelevant, really, because you aren't the boss and, just because the boss is doing something you don't agree with, it doesn't mean that you should have his or her position. Don't moan about the job for years, just do something about it and set up on your own.

Quite often, people start a business to prove something, either to themselves or to someone else. I remember sitting explaining my plan to set up a coaching school. The friend I was telling did not see how it would work. Rather than put me off, it did the exact opposite. I simply thought, 'Here's another person I'm going to prove wrong.' When someone says you can't do it, you say, 'Oh yes I can!' It is a bit childish, really, but it's one hell of a motivator.

Many people actually get into running their own business for the wrong reasons. They do it because they see it providing them with a job as a soft alternative to actually working for someone else. Anyone who is self-employed will tell you it is absolutely not a soft option. Many self-employed people, including me at times, think it would be wonderful to just wake up in the morning, go somewhere, let someone else tell you what to do then go home at half-past five and forget all about it. Someone else has all the worries and you just do your job, keep your head down and enjoy an easy life. But what a *dull* life.

Here is a list of reasons for and against working for yourself versus working for a boss. Check them out and see which appeal more to you. Instantly, you will be able to tell whether you are dissatisfied with corporate life.

WORKING FOR YOURSELF   WORKING FOR YOUR BOSS

PLUS FACTORS

WORKING FOR YOURSELF	WORKING FOR YOUR BOSS
Freedom	Payment each week/month
Independence	Holiday pay
Control over your own future	Company car
Deeper sense of job satisfaction	Health insurance/sick pay
Greater achievement	Redundancy pay

MINUS FACTORS

WORKING FOR YOURSELF	WORKING FOR YOUR BOSS
Working harder	Little control over getting a rise
Longer hours	
Giving up short-term security	Limited control over promotion
Responsibility for everything	Working to someone else's goals
	Paying tax and hating it

So many people go through the revolving door of life on someone else's push and don't put any effort into doing something first. They are the ones who will ask for a pay rise and say, 'Then I'll work harder.' Instead, they should be rewarded for being a hard worker after the work has been done and they have proved themselves. If you want to progress in any career you've got to start taking a degree of responsibility, but the ultimate responsibility is when you have other people working for you. Then you are also responsible for them, so the level of responsibility grows and grows, which is not something to be taken lightly. Some companies just do not realise the responsibility they have. The salary they pay each month may seem a very small amount to them but it pays their employees' mortgages and meets their bills. Relationships break down when there's not enough money to go around because of the stress it can cause, so working for yourself is never an easy option. Am I scaring you yet?

Almost every single one of us has the ability to run his or her own business. I want to inspire and motivate you to do it but I also want you to go into it with your eyes wide open and with the rose-tinted spectacles well and truly off.

Going it alone is a scary business that many people keep putting off for as long as possible. They say, 'I'll get around to it once the kids have gone back to school' or, 'Well, it's getting close to Christmas.' Then, instead of using the New Year to spur them into action, they put it off again because they are going away on holiday. I want to get you so excited about sacking your boss that you will want to do it as soon as you can. When you decide that the time is right, this book will equip you with all the tools and knowledge that you will need to get going.

DO YOU HAVE WHAT IT TAKES?

You have decided that you do not really like working for a boss. Now let's see if you have what it takes to sack your boss and go it alone.

Have a look at the twelve statements I have listed below and tick the ones you agree with. Then add up the number of ticks you have made.

1. You get excited when you think about having your own business ☐
2. You might feel a little nervous but you just know it is the right thing to do ☐
3. You *know* you will be successful, whatever friends and family say ☐
4. You like telling people what to do ☐
5. You are prepared to put in long hours to make your dream a reality ☐
6. You can imagine a future in which people thank you for your product or service because it has made a positive difference to their lives ☐
7. You are prepared to do what it takes – as long as it is ethical/legal – to achieve your dream ☐
8. You don't mind starting at the bottom (such as changing the light bulbs in your office) to get to the top, where you'll be chairing your first board meeting ☐
9. You don't mind meeting new people and selling yourself with confidence ☐
10. You don't mind getting out of your comfort zone and learning new things ☐
11. You don't mind the prospect of eating, drinking and sleeping your idea and waking up in the middle of the night struggling with a problem ☐
12. You are prepared to accept that the people you thought would support you will do the exact opposite ☐

TOTAL ___

How did you do? If you got more than six you really are thinking seriously about getting rid of your boss. If you got nine or more you have obviously been thinking about dumping your boss for a while and you are ready to hire yourself and launch into the wonderful world of self-employment. If you got fewer than six, perhaps you should stay put for a while longer and, as you read on, you will find the information you need to get into a position where, eventually, you can go on and run your own business.

ACTION PLAN

This is the wheel of business success.

WHEEL 1 shows you the skills you will need to run your own business successfully. Later, I will explain in detail each of these vital skills. The following chapters will cover every skill you need to accomplish to be successful once you have sacked your boss, including marketing, sales, professionalism, networking, finance and accounting, forward planning, self-management, setting goals, customer service, paperwork and people management.

Now look at **WHEEL 2**. You will see a scale from one to ten. I would like you to mark yourself out of ten on how good you think you would be at each of these skills. Be very honest with yourself. If you do not know much about marketing, you might give yourself a four for that section, but if you are already extremely good at networking you could give yourself a nine for that area. Perhaps people management is part of your current job and you're quite good at that, so maybe you would score seven there. Finance? You might need help with that, and with paperwork, which has never been your strong point. Attitude? You're always upbeat, say an eight. Then shade in the amount of each segment that represents your abilities. Now look at the shape of the inner wheel you have created. If it is anything like the shape in Wheel Number Two it is probably going to be a bumpy ride.

As you continue to read through this book your knowledge of each subject will increase and, by the time you have reached the end, that inner wheel will start to look a bit smoother. When you do sack your boss and start your own business, you'll become more skilled in the areas where you were weakest. Otherwise, you can always employ some help and then that inner wheel will appear much more rounded.

If you did this exercise every month you would see each segment of your wheel start to move out. The perfect business would have a ten for everything. You are unlikely ever to achieve that but it is good to aim for. Now fill in your wheel. Remember, be honest, otherwise you will only be kidding yourself.

WHEEL 1

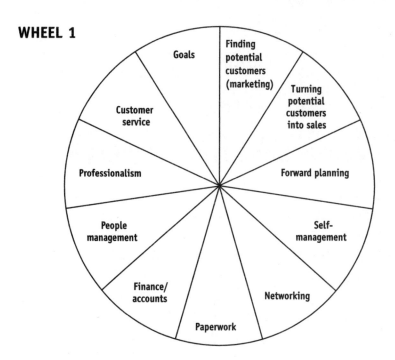

WHEEL 2

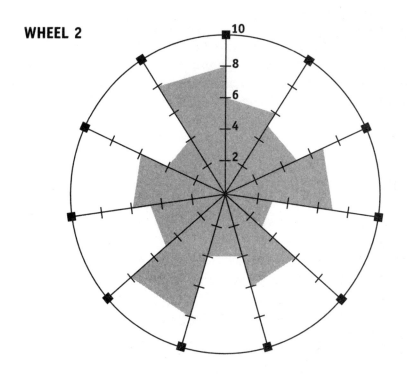

CHAPTER 3

YOU'VE DONE IT! NOW WHAT?

You've done it! You have finally decided you have what it takes to set up your own business. What now?

I'll tell you what *not* to do. Don't charge into the boss's office and slap down your resignation letter. Stop and think. Have you set your goals? Have you thought through exactly how your business will run?

When you've decided that you have to sack your boss, do it by stealth. Once you have decided what sort of business you are going to run, build it up slowly in your spare time and at weekends – it's quite possible. It's not 'do or die'. You don't have to give up everything. Only when you're convinced it will work should you make your move, otherwise the situation could look like this: you tell your boss where to stick his job, quit and walk out; a month later you realise that your fantastic idea isn't quite so clever after all and it's all going horribly wrong. What happens then? It's rather hard to go back, isn't it?

Once you know your business will work, go to your boss and make it very clear that you are going to start on your own. You could even tell them that they have inspired you to do this. How can you be criticised when you have paid them such a compliment? Follow it up with a plea to their better nature: 'I wondered whether I'd be able to phone you occasionally for any help or advice. Likewise, if you want me to help or advise my replacement, I'll be very happy to do so.'

Putting it that way creates a great relationship. For example, if you were setting yourself up as a web designer and you quit your company, someone might mention to your boss that the company needs a new website, at which point, hopefully, you will be uppermost in their mind. So there's no point in making the dramatic exit, no point at all. Although you might not want to, you have got to do it with decorum and professionalism.

When I quit my life as a hypnotist on Ibiza I had no idea what I was going to do, but I knew I wanted the trappings of a business. I wanted an office, I wanted a desk, I wanted a big leather chair and I wanted the staff, but I didn't have very much money because, for the several months I'd been in Ibiza, I'd been spending every penny I earned. So I had to go back and do some more hypnosis shows to support my new life as an entrepreneur before making the career change.

Run your new business alongside your salaried work for a while and, when you know it's working, then sack your boss.

Sometimes, people make a very clean break. They say, 'Right, I'm not going to do *this* any more: I'm going to do *this* instead.' On my coaching courses, I hear people say, 'I'm going to quit my regular job on Monday morning.' 'Oh, no,' I have to tell them, 'don't do that. Run your new business alongside your salaried work for a while and, when you know that it's working, then sack your boss. Don't do it on a whim. You have to prepare a plan and stick to it, otherwise your business will be doomed to failure.'

I remember very distinctly an incident when I was living in a basement flat in Southsea. My bedroom didn't have any windows and the door was a very tight fit. One night I woke up suffocating because there was no air left in the room. It was like being sealed in a coffin. As I awoke, like a landed fish gasping for breath, I realised I had a corker of an idea.

My parents had always encouraged me to go to university. I had wanted to do a joint course of drama and French but, because of my results at English A-level, I was unable to take drama and had to do a full-time French course. Unfortunately, my French was not really up to university standard but at that stage no one had worked that out. Soon, my friend Dan and I were watching *The Six Million Dollar Man* on TV on Monday afternoons instead of attending a very dull French lecture. At the end-of-term exams, the forty women on the course all passed with flying colours, while the seven men all got zero.

It was then I realised that French might not be my strong point. So I started to soft-pedal and didn't turn up for classes. Instead, I used my time in London to check out whether I could make it as a magic act. I realised there were far too many magicians working in the capital so I had to do something a bit different. In the end, I decided on mind reading. I entered a college talent competition and did quite well. I came second to a group of singing rugby players. I'm not quite sure, but the judges might have been slightly biased. I remember my friend, Claire, whom I've never seen since, saying she was really proud of me. Little things like that start to add up towards the self-belief you need to be an entrepreneur. Remember the negatives but it is much more important to focus on the positives.

After that limited success, I started developing a mind-reading act. I was never very successful at it because it had the feel of an old music hall act that doesn't really work. The only person who could make a mind-reading act entertaining is Graham Jolley, a fantastic person who lent me £250 about a year after I left university. That £250 saved my life. I have never forgotten his generosity and I have since tried to repay his kindness by booking him for after-dinner performances at the Coaching Academy's events. He now charges £2,500 a night and he's worth every penny.

No one was going to pay a lot to see my act. I had the right idea but the product was not what people wanted. Then, some time before Paul McKenna started appearing on TV, I saw a hypnotism performance at university. It was the most amazing show I had ever seen in my life. I had discovered a product that people really did want. The hypnotist was absolutely outstanding and, to this day, he is still the best I've ever seen – and I have seen a lot of them. He was incredibly funny without being crude. He had real respect for his volunteers' feelings and would never humiliate them.

I hung out with him for years and learned all his secrets for a successful act. Eventually, he suggested I should go out and do my own shows, so I did. I loved college audiences, so I got myself booked onto the university circuit. When my friend tried to get student venues they already had a hypnotist on their books – me. I ended up doing more shows than he did, at a higher rate. We fell out after he phoned me and said, 'I'm going to break your legs. Get out of my venues.' It was such a shame.

I knew the university circuit well. I knew about entertainment. I knew comedians, bands and show-business agents. I also knew, because most of the university entertainment managers had told me, that I had the best promotional material. I did it myself but my material was still more eye-catching than anything other people produced, and it got sales, which is what it's all about, and it gave me a cracking idea. This was to create a magazine and sell advertising space to bands and comedians, in fact anyone in showbiz, as well as people who did bouncy castles and fairground rides. We would then distribute the magazine free of charge to all universities around the country. I worked it out that it would be cheaper for entertainers to put an advertisement in my magazine and have it distributed than to post their own promotional material to hundreds of universities around the country. What is more, it was probably more likely to be read.

I know it is a cliché but you really do learn much more from your mistakes.

Those early days were an amazing education. I know it is a cliché but you really do learn much more from your mistakes. It was when my brother Charles and I rented an office by the month in a big draughty building in Portsmouth that I made my first.

It's a mistake that many new businesses make. I was obsessed with the trappings of an office. In the early days, I spent more time rearranging furniture than actually doing any business. I was constantly saying, 'I think we should have the filing cabinet over there and move the two desks together.' It just was not important, but it was easy to get distracted because it seemed more important to impress people with my office than create an impact with a successful business.

One day, a photocopier salesman called Harry Jarbath walked into the office. He was a dynamic New Yorker living in Portsmouth and he easily convinced me that our fledgling business needed a photocopier. Stupidly, I entered into a three-year agreement with Xerox. When you sign a contract like that you never get out of it, so, for two and a half years, I had a photocopier that I didn't want and I was paying hand over fist for it. It was one of my major expenses and later, when I was short of money and counting every penny, I still had to pay Xerox. It's not a case of stopping paying it and their coming and picking up the photo-copier. They will come and pick up the photocopier, then sue you for the balance.

Signing long-term contracts very early in a business is a bad idea. It is like getting married on a first date. You don't do it. You don't want long-term commitment at that stage: you want to see how it goes and get comfortable with it first. Harry the supersalesman and I became rea-sonably good acquaintances. Soon after selling me the photocopier, Harry bought a massive five-bedroom Victorian semidetached in Southsea. I went round to see him when he moved in. It was a beauti-ful house but way out of my league. That's when I said, 'Harry I'd love to have a house like this one day.' Three years later, it became mine. I bought it from Harry when he and his family moved back to the United States – but ended up living alone in a five-bedroom house and hated it. So be careful what you wish for when setting your goals – they really do come true.

TIP

Persistence is the key to success. If you do not believe that your new business is going to be successful, then you might just as well not start it. If you have doubts, don't do it. If you hold an unshakeable self-belief, then you will be successful and that is worth more than anything else. If you can hold your head high, look someone straight in the eye and speak with confidence, then people will say, 'Wow, he really believes in himself!' It will propel you to the forefront because no one is going to give the opportunity to someone who doubts him- or herself. It is just not going to happen. I have wavered only once, just for a few moments, seconds, really, when I was faced with a huge pile of bills. I held my head in my hands and wondered whether I was doing the right thing.

People give up too easily in business. They quit when they are just moments from success, so never realise it. If you give up too easily you will never know what you might have won. The persistent ones will succeed. Look at James Dyson of vacuum cleaner fame. He is an incredible example of persistence. He remortgaged his house, again and again and again. A large vacuum manufacturer ripped off his idea for a bagless vacuum cleaner but he did not give up. Now look at him: he's a highly successful multimillionaire.

ACTION PLAN

List thirty people you could contact in the next seven days who will be able to help you in your quest to start your own business. They may be people with whom you can sound out your ideas and others who can help get your venture off the ground.

1. _____   16. _____
2. _____   17. _____
3. _____   18. _____
4. _____   19. _____
5. _____   20. _____
6. _____   21. _____
7. _____   22. _____
8. _____   23. _____
9. _____   24. _____
10. _____   25. _____
11. _____   26. _____
12. _____   27. _____
13. _____   28. _____
14. _____   29. _____
15. _____   30. _____

You have joined the Sack Your Boss Revolution. You have decided to quit paid employment and try working for yourself, and you will never regret it if you follow my wheel of business success. The chapters that follow take each segment of the wheel and show you how to develop the skills you need to succeed.

" SETTING UP
YOUR
BUSINESS "

CHAPTER 4

SELF-MANAGEMENT

Get rid of your stinking thinking. You need a positive attitude when you sack your boss and become self-employed. It will mean a complete change in thinking and outlook because, if you are going to be your own boss, you will need to get out of your comfort zone. Some people have incredibly small comfort zones. Some people simply can't move out of this space. They won't speak to someone they don't know; they will not eat in a restaurant they haven't tried; they won't go to a new holiday destination (how did they get to any holiday destination in the first place? I wonder). They will never do anything that is different, and you cannot get any more different than running your own business.

Brian Tracy, who has written several books dealing with positive attitude, tells an amazing story of identical twin boys. Even though they look the same, their personalities are totally different. Johnny is very, very positive. He is everyone's friend and loves life. He is so inspired he's practically a danger to himself. Jimmy, on the other hand, is a born whinger. Totally negative, he is never happy or content. Nothing in his life is good enough.

Their parents have become concerned, so they conduct an experiment at Christmas to see if they can balance out the boys' personalities. The pair come downstairs on Christmas morning to find a pile of presents under the tree. Every single package is for Jimmy. True to form, he finds fault with each one: it is not the correct size, not the right colour or he just simply doesn't like it. Johnny waits patiently as his grumpy brother works his way through the huge pile of gifts. Finally, he asks his parents, 'Do I get a present?' 'Yes,' they reply. 'It's out in the garage.' Johnny opens the doors of their huge double garage to be confronted by a mountain of horse dung.

The parents go back into the house, hoping Johnny will at last explode with anger and turn on his whingeing brother but, after an hour, Johnny still hasn't come back in. They return to the garage to find the boy burrowing in the manure. Horrified, they ask, 'What on earth are you doing?' Covered from head to foot in dung, Johnny explains, 'Well, with all this horse manure there has to be a pony in there somewhere!'

The moral of the story is that, when you go it alone, however much horse manure there is in your life, there's always a pony in there somewhere.

What drives you to get up in the morning? Will you still have the motivation to get up when no one is going to be tapping their watch and tutting if you are late for work? Will you be able to get into your own office for nine o'clock when there is no one looking over your shoulder? *Your attitude will play a major part in your success.*

I have set out below how attitude can lead to 100 per cent success. The number beside each letter of the word 'attitude' represents the letter's place in the alphabet. Amazingly, when you add up the values of all the letters in 'attitude', the total comes to 100.

1	**A** – Action-oriented
20	**T** – Take responsibility
20	**T** – Turn negative into positive
9	**I** – Imitate excellence
20	**T** – Turn fear into focus
21	**U** – Uncover your hidden talents
4	**D** – Develop yourself
5	**E** – Expect the unexpected
100	**Attitude = 100 per cent of success**

The word 'attitude' also spells out all the attributes you will need when you start to work for yourself.

ACTION ORIENTATION

There are three types of people:

- the person who talks about things;

- the person who makes things happen; and

- the person who asks, 'What happened?'

Once you have sacked your boss, you have to become the person who makes things happen. Entrepreneurs get things done. If there's a problem, if there is a challenge, there is always a way round it – every single time. It may not be the perfect solution but there is always a solution. To be the person who makes things happen you need self-belief and self-motivation, because all around you people will be telling you, 'Oh, you can't do that!' *You have to believe you can do it.*

You are probably asking, 'How do I get that self-belief?' The answer is that it comes from small successes. You start to believe that you can do something and, with each success, you develop more self-belief. It's a snowball effect and eventually you become more resilient to negativity and build a protective shell around yourself. Negative feelings and failure can stick, so you need to shake them off. Don't let failure hold you back. Use it to keep you humble, but do not let it stop you from trying again and again.

When I was at school, my economics teacher wrote on my end-of-sixth-form report, 'I wish Jonathan luck. He'll certainly need it.' I have never met him again but the irony is that I actually went back to my old school, years later, to talk to the sixth form – about success! The important thing was that I did not allow his negativity to get me down.

You need to develop a thick skin. I know it is hard. During filming on a TV show in Barcelona, the sound engineer told me, 'You're the worst presenter I've ever seen.' It was a joke and, in the context, it was funny, but later I started thinking, 'Did he mean that?' It is so easy to start doubting yourself, so positive praise and encouragement is really important.

Support from your family and work colleagues is vital as well. It is such a shame when people don't have it from their immediate family. If your partner doesn't support and encourage you in your new venture, you should not be with that person. Quite often, they get jealous and try to bring you down. They want to keep you level with them and, if this is the problem with your partner, that person is quite simply not right for you.

TAKE RESPONSIBILITY

If you don't take responsibility for your own life, no one else will. Getting out of the idea that if you don't show up for work for a few days you still get paid is a real culture shock. A lot of people who start their own businesses act as though they were on holiday. When you start your own business you have got to expect to work twice as hard as when you worked for someone else, because now the buck stops with you.

You can't simply pass the problem on to someone else in another department. Whether you like it or not, you are responsible for everything, the good stuff and the bad, and, believe me, in the early days of running your own business there is a lot of bad stuff. There is a lot of good stuff too, such as taking responsibility for your successes. It is great when someone says, 'Well done!' You can actually look them straight in the eye and say, 'Thank you very much' rather than 'Oh, well, it's nothing.'

Some people think entrepreneurs are arrogant. It's not arrogance: it's self-belief and self-confidence. However, the entrepreneur should also be able to say, 'I messed up big time and it's my fault.'

Two years ago, I thought it would be a great idea to run a one-day conference for our customers followed by an evening dinner-dance. I hired the InterContinental Hotel at Hyde Park in London, not one of the cheapest venues. I booked four speakers, one of whom flew in from Australia at great expense, and hired an eight-piece band. I also booked a comedy speaker to follow the three-course dinner, and Graham Jolley, the mind reader I mentioned earlier. Tickets for the evening were not expensive for a day and an evening event but, in spite of that, they were really hard work to sell. When everything was added up I lost £25,000. I might as well have piled up £25,000 in notes and set fire to them.

I got carried away and tried to create something too grand. What I should have done was advertise the tickets to see how many sold in the first week. If you can't sell tickets for an event in the first week, don't bother doing it. I could have quietly buried it but, by committing to substantial expenses, including the band at £3,000, the PA equipment at £1,000 and the entertainer at another £2,500, I had to cover an absolute fortune. It was awful, absolutely awful. When, much later, you need £25,000, you look back and think, 'If I hadn't done that I would have that twenty-five grand now.'

It's very easy to get things wrong, but you can't afford to get *too* many things wrong at the start. You would think that I would have learned my lesson from that experience, but no: four months later, I did it all over again, this time losing only about £10,000. I took responsibility for it and did not do it again. Finally, I'd learned my lesson.

You also have to be responsible for your staff. When I first embarked on my new venture, I paid my staff £7,000 a year and I wondered why I wasn't getting results. I realised it was because I had £7,000-a-year employees. I was paying rock-bottom wages and suffering as a result. I remember that at one sales meeting I wanted to know why we were not selling enough advertising space in our magazine. That was when I discovered that you will hear every excuse under the sun for people's failure to achieve. The best excuse I ever heard from a salesperson was, 'I think it could be the chairs. They aren't very comfortable and that's why we're not selling.'

One of our coaches who did some sales work for us at the Coaching Academy was Emil Raal, a South African, who is one of the most well-rounded individuals I've ever met in terms of taking responsibility for himself. I once asked him, 'Emil, why do you think it's not going so well for you at the moment?' He replied, 'I think maybe it's me.' He actually admitted the fault might lie with him, rather than external circumstances. He took responsibility, and that was brilliant.

How can you take responsibility for other people's lives if you cannot take responsibility for your own?

TIP

When you are starting out in business, you need an agreement with everyone who works for you and with you. In the early days, people will give a lot of their time, skills and knowledge, quite often for nothing. But, when you become successful, they will want to be recompensed. Your agreement needs to set out exactly what their contribution will be and what they will be paid. If someone is going to give you a day of their time, you don't want them to come back in a year's time saying, 'All those ideas I gave you on that day are obviously part of the business now. I think I'm owed 20 per cent of your company.'

It does happen, and I know, because it happened to me. People come out of the woodwork and claim part of your success. They think they have rights over your business when it is you who have done all the donkey work. It is absolutely vital that there be a written agreement because, if terms are agreed on a handshake, a year later you won't remember accurately what you discussed. It doesn't have to be done by a lawyer: it can be a simple letter agreeing what each party will do as their part of the arrangement and how the money will be split. You both sign and each person keeps a copy. Then, if there is a dispute, you can refer to your copy.

Do not take a partner is my advice to anyone who wants to go it alone. Do it by yourself if you can. It is not in the entrepreneurial spirit to take on partners and you should not be accumulating people at this early stage. As I said earlier, there will be endless squabbles about who is in charge. You are all equal partners, so who's going to be the managing director?

'I think I should be.'

'I think you should be.'

'I think she should be.'

'Oh, we'll all be joint managing directors!'

It doesn't work. That doesn't mean those people can't play their part, but they should contribute on a contractual basis. For example, you might need to hire someone to do the accounts for one day a week in return for a fee, in which case that is all that is involved in the relationship.

TURN NEGATIVE INTO POSITIVE

I used to fall out with people endlessly, including staff and suppliers. I used always to think I'd been overcharged, whatever the amount owed. I kept such a tight hold on the purse strings that I didn't like paying people. I fell out with one of my staff because I didn't think she was being productive enough. Six and a half years later, I was asked out for Christmas drinks and ended up sitting next to her, so I made a big apology, which is always easier after a few glasses of wine. I said, 'Look, I think I treated you very badly back then and I just want to say I'm sorry, and ask if I can make it up to you in any way.' I know it made me feel better and I hope she forgave me.

TIP

I always paid my suppliers at the end of the following month. So, depending on when they sent in an invoice, some were waiting nearly 60 days to be paid. Then I told them all that I would pay every bill within seven days, in exchange for a 2.5 per cent reduction in the invoice. They would be paid more quickly and I saved money. On my turnover at the time, that saving of 2.5 per cent amounted to one person's salary for the whole year.

IMITATE EXCELLENCE

Learn from other businesses. You should watch everything your rivals do. If they do something well, imitate it. We can all learn from people in other business. You could even start a Mastermind Group, which involves teaming up with several business owners not in competition with you (you do not want to share your trade secrets with your competitors) in order to learn from each other, brainstorm ideas and talk about your challenges. You might go to the group, for example, and say, 'I had this problem with an employee and needed to reprimand him, so I checked out the law and this is what you have to do to comply with the regulations'; or, 'I can't seem to get people to pay me on time. What would the group recommend?' You can learn from the best bits of each other's business and enjoy mutual support in this way. You can check out a lot more on networking on page 86.

TURN FEAR INTO FOCUS

We all fear failure. That is what drives us on, every day. Part of the 'fun' of running your own business is conquering the fear that it will all go wrong. One of the best books on coaching is called *The Inner Game of Tennis*. It was written by a tennis coach who realised his students' performances were not based just on how they held the racket or how they moved around the court. It was 'the inner game' inside their heads that actually influenced the result. Sportsmen and -women who achieve what appear to be absolutely remarkable feats of skill admit that they play out the scenario in their mind's eye over and over again. It is called *visualisation*, and you visualise the outcome of a situation. In my head, I always 'practised' what it would feel like to succeed, and I knew exactly what I would feel, even before it happened.

I did this in a very small way with my driving test. I was such a bad driver that my driving instructor said he'd have to take me off the road, but I visualised myself driving perfectly and, on the day, I passed. So take a couple of minutes every day to visualise what you want. It could be anything. It could be something to do with your business or it could even be making a relationship work. Visualisation makes your goals more real.

UNCOVER YOUR HIDDEN TALENTS

Play to your strengths. You do not have to set up a business that is in the line of work you have always been in. Nowadays we have several careers in our working lifetime, so you can develop a new skill and turn it into your business. It may be a talent you have not recognised, or perhaps people around you have told you that you are good at something, such as interior design. Sacking your boss is a chance to do something completely different and challenging, so listen to those around you who often will recognise your hidden talent before you.

DEVELOP YOURSELF

Never stop learning. I am a great believer in learning lessons, but that does not mean you have constantly to go on courses. You should continue to learn from everyone and everything around you to improve your business. Never think you know all there is to know about your line of business, as there is always something you can add to your experience. For example, I am constantly learning new things about marketing, although I am very experienced in the area.

EXPECT THE UNEXPECTED

Everything always costs far more than you think, and you will make a fraction of the money you expect. Sitting bang in the middle between those polar opposites are your bills. The bills are always higher and you always have less money in your bank account than you think, so you start juggling bills. In the early days, new business owners become very good bill jugglers. You need to weigh up which bills are important and which are not but, the more you put off paying your bills, the scarier it becomes.

If you think that, by hiding away the invoice in a drawer, it will go away, know now that it won't, which of course is the very reason established companies are very wary of doing business with new firms. Will the business still be around long enough for them to get paid? The longer you leave a bill unpaid the bigger it gets. If you don't pay your suppliers they will add interest plus debt-collection charges and, before you know it, you are paying 10 or 20 per cent more than the initial bill.

So there you have it: the word 'attitude' summarises the differences between the successful entrepreneur and the failure.

CHAPTER 5

FINANCE AND ACCOUNTS

One thing I wish I had done right at the start was to get myself a good accountant.

Some time ago, someone recommended his accountant to me. I should have known better than to follow it up because the recommendation came from a street entertainer who dealt with very small amounts of money. He took two- and ten-pence pieces in his hat and his accountant was seriously dodgy. He never answered his phone for a start, always a worrying sign. He was also hopeless. I don't think he had any qualifications.

I should have been suspicious when he insisted on coming round to my office to work on the figures. Alarm bells should certainly have started ringing when I saw his prices. He was just too cheap. He did the work for £25 and, when he asked for payment, I said 'OK, that's fine, but could you send an invoice?' As the boss of my new company, I always enjoyed saying, 'Send me your invoice'! That is when he replied, 'You couldn't pay me in cash now, could you? I need to go shopping.' So I upgraded to someone else.

What I really needed was a bookkeeper rather than an accountant – someone who would come in once a week, even for a couple of hours, to look at all the bits of paper I had collected, put them in order and file them. The worst thing is to try to do it yourself because you will be taking your eye off the all-important sales and marketing ball, the lifeblood of your business. What usually happens is that, because you hate the paperwork so much, you simply ignore it. Then suddenly business starts to pick up, which causes even more paperwork, and you are so focused on the new business that you forget the accounts altogether. At the end of the year you will have carrier bags full of receipts and sales invoices and it becomes such a dreadful mess that your accountant is forced to charge you twice as much to sort it all out.

It's better to have someone in for a couple of hours every single week just to type it all up and keep it on a spreadsheet so you don't have to worry about it. You will have more than enough to worry about from the Inland Revenue and Customs and Excise. They are not forgiving people. You can't say, 'I was too busy' or 'My mother was very ill', because they don't believe you and they don't care, anyway. You may in fact be telling the truth but they are not going to excuse anyone, otherwise they wouldn't be able to do the Queen's business and collect all that revenue for the government.

When you start making money you realise you have to give nearly half of it away.

When you start making money you realise you have to give nearly half of it away and, personally, I think that the tax system is outrageous. I don't mind contributing to the running of the country but I hate the thought that, the harder I work, the more I have to give to the Treasury. I don't think I would ever do it but I can understand why people become tax exiles. (You will find more details about tax and VAT on pages 76–7.)

If things go wrong, you need an accountant who will not only help you to sort out the mess but one who will coach you as well. You need him or her to say, 'OK, let's have a look at this situation and see how we got ourselves here,' and, more importantly, 'How we can avoid its happening again in the future.' Very few accountants do that but I am lucky to have one who does and Rob Rendle has been an enormous contributor to the growth of my business. In fact, it was his encouragement that motivated me to write this book.

Do not borrow too much money when you start your business. Whenever I talk to business schools, students always ask me, 'How do you get finance? How do you raise the money?' Because they are academic entrepreneurs, they are obsessed with raising a pot of money as start-up capital to spend on this and that, before they have even made their first sale. This is not how you do it in real life. The last thing you want to do is to start your business life with a debt. It is like a couple getting married with a £10,000 loan to cover the cost of the wedding and a further £5,000 loan for the honeymoon. Why start married life with a £15,000 debt? It is completely wrong. Won't there be enough stress already?

The same applies to business. You should say, 'Look, we can't afford a holiday just yet, but let's go away for a weekend and, once the business is really up and running, then we can go away as much as we want.' You will feel so much more satisfaction when you take your first holiday paid for out of your profits, rather than your overdraft.

TIP

One of the wonderful things my financial director has introduced is a weekly financial health check for the company. By lunchtime every Monday, I receive a folder containing a complete breakdown of the previous week's trading. I can see exactly what has happened in terms of sales and what business was created in pounds and pence, how much money we banked and what our VAT and PAYE liabilities are. I know what our debtors owe and how much we have to pay our creditors. Rob calls it 'The Academy at a Glance'. It started out as an A4 sheet but, as time has gone on, it has been expanded to include a more detailed sales-and-marketing analysis. It is the only true way of knowing exactly how your company is performing. If you ask your staff, 'Did we have a good week?' you will not get a realistic picture. They will say things such as, 'Oh, yes, but it was a bit quiet towards the end of the week.' Then you get the figures and discover it was far from quiet at the end of the week because a hundred new enquires were made on Thursday. When you enquire further you find the person you asked was not actually in on Thursday. Get the real facts and the figures because conjecture is not reliable.

ACTION PLAN

If finance and bookkeeping are not your strong points, work out now whom you are going to get in to keep your finances in order. Do not neglect it until it is too late. Act now and think about whom you can hire. You may need them for only a couple of hours a week at first.

CASH FLOW

The business plan I put together for my magazine had one serious flaw. Yes, we could sell advertising space but, by the second issue of the *Student Entertainment Guide*, I realised that getting paid was proving to be a real problem.

Typically with magazines, customers pay on publication for the advertising they have bought, but printers want to be paid up front, especially by new companies such as mine. So I had to pay the printer in advance. After funding two editions, I thought, 'Great, now I'll get in money from my advertisers.' I now know from bitter experience that advertisers are extremely wily when it comes to avoiding payment. 'Well, I requested a right-hand page and you gave me a left,' they might moan, or they'd argue, 'I wanted spot colour and I only got black and white.' They might say, 'I was right next to one of my competitors. I didn't want that.' Then they would try, 'It's come out a bit blurry on my copy.' 'Well, yours is the only one that's like that,' I'd reply in desperation, to which they would say, 'I'm only going to pay you half!' I must have heard every excuse under the sun why a bill shouldn't be paid.

I quickly realised that getting all these bands and comedians to advertise with us was a brilliant idea but they did not have much money. They may have had money in their pockets when they booked the advertisement but, three months later when it was time to pay, they hadn't any left. You can threaten to pursue them through the courts but they turn to you and say, 'Fine, sue me.' You are still no nearer getting your money and then you have to start paying expensive lawyers' bills.

Someone who owed £1,800 sent me a cheque for £1 and offered to pay £1 a month. It was not worth pursuing because it would have taken 150 years to clear the debt. After two issues of the *Student Entertainment Guide*, I realised no one was going to pay.

I began to think about the problem and ask myself, 'Who has money in entertainment?' Corporate event organisers, I answered, that's who. So the *Business Entertainment Guide* was born. It needed to be a colour magazine, which meant that my costs rose dramatically. If I were doing it again, I would probably make it an online publication with no print costs but, of course, that's with the benefit of hindsight. We started selling advertising space to businesses and we did get paid, but it was an incredibly competitive market, as everyone was after the corporates because these customers had a substantial advertising budget.

After two or three issues, my brother Charles and I realised that either we should delay publication for weeks until we had sold the advertising – which, of course, would make our advertisers nervous – or we should do something different. Our main cost was printing, and one Monday the printer phoned and demanded that I pay his bill. I asked him to give me a little longer. That was when he got really angry and warned me that if I didn't settle by Friday he would bankrupt me. Maybe he was short of money himself but it was a damn scary thing to hear.

So I thought, 'Right, fine, we'll pay this, whatever it takes' – and I did. One of the things I did was sell my office furniture, including the chair I was sitting on. Then I phoned all the people who owed me money. I told them I needed a cheque right now. It is amazing how, quite often when you are owed money, your debtors are not being difficult: they just have a policy of not paying until they are asked. It is a bit odd but some companies do that. I still use the same printer today. He is a great printer and does a fantastic job. He has probably forgotten the conversation, but things like that stick with you always.

It was time for lateral thinking. To produce a 36-page magazine we had to sell a certain amount of advertising space to make it pay. Did it have to be a 36-page magazine? So we came up with an A5, landscape, spiral-bound booklet. Then as a real stroke of genius – I have no idea who thought of it – inside the back cover we included a tear-out Freepost postcard, which meant that, if a reader wanted more information on any advertiser, they simply circled the name on the postcard and posted it. It was a perfect idea because, when the postcard came back, we would phone the advertiser and say, 'We've got six people here who are interested in your services but I notice you haven't paid your bill.' So our customers did not get their sales leads until they had paid.

Building up a reputation right from the start for honest, straight, ethical dealing is essential.

TIP

Create a business in which you get paid in advance. Do not deliver anything until you get paid. If you can run a company with no bad debts and without being owed money, then you are laughing. It is also important to build up a good relationship with your suppliers right from the start. Even if your printing bill is only £50, pay on time every single month. Then, after three or four months, ask your supplier, 'Could you write me a letter explaining that, over the last four months, I have always paid you on time and that you have never had to hassle me for it?'

Just imagine if you had a dozen of those letters. When you wanted to open an account with a potential supplier who needs trade references before offering credit, you could say, 'No problem, here are a dozen letters.' It's reassuring. Building up a reputation right from the start for honest, straight, ethical dealing is essential. You might be an honest, straight, ethical person inside but that's not good enough. You have to demonstrate your honesty with evidence rather than hope people will believe you. With letters from existing suppliers, you are saying, 'Not only am I honest and I'll pay you, but here are twelve people with whom I do business who can prove it.'

Don't go on beating your head against a brick wall. Too many people give up too easily and quit just as they are about to make their big breakthrough. However, while you should never quit, as an entrepreneur you must also not throw good money after bad. Always remember that it is your money. I realised quickly that neither of my free magazines was going to take off in the way I wanted, and there was nothing to be gained from persisting to the point of stupidity. The definition of insanity is to keep on doing the same thing and expecting different results.

I loved the personal-development industry. Avidly, I read books by people such as Tony Robbins, Jay Abraham, Brian Tracy and a man called Maxwell Maltz, who wrote an amazing book on self-belief. The whole subject of personal development made a big impact on me. There were no personal-development magazines on the market, so I decided to set up my own. One of my motivations was purely selfish. I wanted to meet all these people I had come to know through their books. Having a magazine can open so many doors and, as a publisher, I could just call them up and they would talk to me. By now I had become a lot more 'savvy' about marketing. I realised from my two free magazines that making money from publishing was very difficult. I was going to charge for this magazine and make money from the cover price, rather than from the advertising alone. I charged a subscription of £195 for twelve issues.

Most of the advertising came from contra deals, which meant swapping products. Barter costs you nothing and it gets you far more in return. When you are starting your business, why not save money by swapping your services? If you are going to set up as a graphic designer, why not approach a printer and say, 'Look, I'll design your new corporate identity if you'll do my printing'? I would advertise personal-development seminars in return for a mention of my magazine in the advertiser's client newsletter. We did not call it a magazine: instead it was referred to as the *Achievement Report*, which sounded more expensive.

However, I did produce it as a colour magazine, which was a mistake. It should have been a black-and-white newsletter with a very simple layout. People expect to pay more for newsletters because they contain inside information on their industry. Personal-development experts wrote for the *Achievement Report* and every month we would hold related seminars with an entrance fee. This spin-off was to be one that eventually turned into the business I now have. I started making more money from organising seminars than publishing the magazine.

Now, how is this for turning a negative into a positive? On the day the first issue of my personal-development magazine was published, I was attending a Tony Robbins seminar at the Islington Design Centre in London, where one of my magazines was on display. Someone walking by picked up a copy of the *Achievement Report*, flicked through it and asked the price. I told him that it was £195 for twelve issues and he replied, 'It's not worth it – it's a waste of money. Who publishes it?' I could have been rude back to him but he may have had a point. Instead, I got into conversation with this man, Rex Sumner, who runs a company specialising in direct mail.

We've since become good friends and he still does a lot of work for us. In fact, it was Rex who introduced me to Mark Rimmington, who ran a company called Bright Ideas, organisers of seminars on personal development. He used to bring speakers over from the States. He would hire a room and sell tickets to people who wanted to hear his speakers. Over the years, Mark had built up a database of 12,000 people who had not only been to his seminars but who also had a track record of spending money on personal development. Mark let me contact these people about the *Achievement Report* and I got some subscriptions from it.

One day, he asked if he could take over a couple of my seminar slots at the Personal Development Show at Olympia. The speaker he wanted to put on was an American, Laura Berman Fortgang, who would be speaking about life coaching. Sportsmen and -women have used coaches to help improve their performance for decades. A coach can achieve exactly the same results with your life. Life coaching originated in the United States. It works on the principle that everything is a lot easier when there is someone working with you to provide encouragement and motivation. You will get to where you want to go faster than you would if you were doing it alone.

Whatever your goal in life, a coach can help you achieve it. Whether it is getting a promotion, going for a job or running your business, a coach can keep you motivated and on track. Perhaps you feel your life is heading in the wrong direction, or you would like to get a better balance in your life. The coach will help you to plan a strategy to take you where you want to go. The results are incredibly powerful because it is hard to go through that process on your own. Laura Berman Fortgang had just written a book called *Take Yourself to the Top* and there had been an article about it in the *Mail on Sunday*'s *You* magazine. As a result, the seminar was packed out. The audience were crammed into the auditorium. Two hundred people occupied the seats and another hundred were sitting in the aisles. It was a health-and-safety nightmare but people just wanted to see this woman. As my part of the deal, Laura signed copies of her book on my stand and I was allowed to video her talk, which I gave away free to anyone who took out a subscription to the *Achievement Report*. I learned later that 400 of the people who had gone along to see Laura Berman Fortgang actually wanted to become coaches themselves. That was an interesting statistic and it made me aware that there was obviously a demand here.

The seeds of an idea started to form. I had definitely spotted a gap in the market. There is no one key to success. It is more like a combination lock in which the tumblers have to fall into place. You have to find a product and a market, then comes timing. So often you can have a great idea but the timing is not right. Perhaps the market is not ready for it or you're in the wrong location. At last, the tumblers were all falling into place to unlock my door to success. The following Monday night, I went to see Laura speak in London. Again, the audience loved her and I was incredibly impressed. Afterwards, I asked her whether she would consider an arrangement whereby she would give me the licence to use her name. I would open the Laura Berman Fortgang Coach Training School in the United Kingdom. She did not even need to think about it. She said 'no' instantly.

I had not quite cracked the combination but I did not give up either. I set about doing more research to find out all I could about the coaching industry. The other crazy coincidence was that, for the three days of the Olympia show, my *Achievement Report* stand was opposite an American coaching school, staffed by their British students. Talking to them, I discovered that theirs was the only coach-training school in the UK.

Doing research into coaching took my mind off my money worries. I would go home late from the office to my one-bedroom flat to be greeted by a sea of final demands that I could not pay. I was putting every penny I had into the *Achievement Report* and completely neglecting my personal life. One night, I remember sitting down on the sofa, putting my head in my hands and crying because I just could not see how the situation was going to get any better. My home phone had been cut off and I was three months in arrears with my mortgage. Because the phone had been disconnected, the bank had to write to let me know that, if the arrears were not settled, they would be forced to repossess the flat.

I was still doing the occasional hypnotism show and I picked up a cheque for £600 from a college in Cambridge. Did I pay it into my private account? If I had, it would have covered the mortgage and I'd be back on track. Instead, I paid it into the business account because that meant more to me. Then I went through every option I could think of to survive. What would happen if I gave up the office and worked from home? I got my flat valued and calculated that, if I sold it, I could pay off all my debts and be back on the straight and narrow, but I would have nowhere to live. I did eventually sell the flat but I now wish I had not, since property prices in that area have gone through the roof, but I had to make a decision and I survived. Even in my darkest hour, I had enough self-belief to know it would work out right. It would happen.

In the end, I did not have long to wait. In July 1999, one month after the show at Olympia, Tony Robbins was hosting a big event in Cardiff at which thousands of people were expected. I contacted the organisers and offered them a free advert in the *Achievement Report* if I could take my magazine along and promote it at the event. Again, everyone I met at Cardiff seemed to be talking about coaching. When you are focused on something you see it everywhere. Just as when you buy a new car and suddenly everywhere you go you see that same type of car, people who are looking for opportunities see openings everywhere. Conversely, people who are looking for problems will find only problems. You get what you focus on.

I was by now obsessed with coaching. I drove back from the Tony Robbins event, went straight to the office and wrote the advertising copy for what was to become the British Coaching Academy, to differentiate it from the American school. I still have the advertisement and, looking at it five years later, I see it was inspired (if I say so myself!). It was a great example of how you can start a business with no money or even an overdraft nudging £20,000. I wrote the advertising copy, which ran to six pages, and then I racked my brains. What do I do? What can I do?

I knew Mark Rimmington's mailing list of 12,000 names now included the 500 people who went to Laura Berman Fortgang's seminar and I knew 400 of those were interested in training to become coaches. So I called in a favour and told Mark I wanted to put something in his next mailing. I spent £145 I hadn't got having 10,000 postcards printed, which said, 'Have you got what it takes to become a personal coach?' followed by some snappy marketing copy:

The British Coaching Academy

Have you got what it takes to become a personal coach?

Personal coaching is the new era of personal development and for the coach it offers a profession that is enjoyable, flexible and highly profitable.

If you are a 'people person', becoming a personal coach could be the best move you've ever made. The hours are flexible and there are high rewards for hard work.

The British Coaching Academy trains people to be professional coaches. If you are a good listener and are of a generally positive nature, can communicate well and can get people to 'open up to you' then maybe you should request more information. Becoming a coach can be a career change or an additional income but, whatever hours you choose to work, you will get the satisfaction of knowing you are helping people attain their goals.

You will work on a one-to-one basis with people from all walks of life and have weekly contact with your clients over the telephone. You will guide them through life's challenges and help them reach their goals faster and faster.

To request more information about becoming a personal coach, fill in your details overleaf and return to us.

I couldn't even afford to fund a Freepost address. Anyone replying had to use a stamp and send their response to a smart mailing address I had rented at Bedford Square in London, from where the mail was forwarded to us in Portsmouth. While I was waiting for Mark to send out my newsletter and postcard, I was forced to sell my car. I had taken the Ford Escort to the garage for repair, which, to my horror, was going to cost £1,500. That was the amount the car was worth, so I sold it to the garage and took a cheque for £1,500 straight to the bank. The money simply disappeared into the overdraft but the car had been on hire purchase and I still had about £10,000 left to pay back. Making repayments on something I didn't even own any more was absolutely crazy.

By now my bank manager was phoning me daily, reminding me, 'Jonathan, you're nudging your overdraft limit.' When you are worried about money, it affects your whole life. Your relationships with the people around you become strained to breaking point. My girlfriend at the time was extremely supportive but I must have been awful to live with because, as well as juggling my finances to stay afloat, I had become obsessed with coaching. I was desperate but I just knew something was going to happen to turn the whole thing around.

Just days after sending out the postcards offering coach training, we were swamped with hundreds and hundreds of enquiries. I did include a Freephone number and the calls went through to a centre where staff took messages and faxed them through to our office. The phones just went crazy and life in our office was absolutely wild. There were only Lisa Snape – the graphic designer on the newsletter – and myself to deal with the deluge of responses. The original copy I'd written for the British Coaching Academy had been set out as an eight-page letter. We photocopied it at the front desk of the business centre and bound the pages together to make a brochure for everyone who applied for more information. We borrowed some kids and they stuffed the brochures into envelopes. Once people received the brochure they started to phone and ask questions before signing up for our first training course. Business just rolled in and, within a matter of days, twenty people had paid £2,000 each.

One of my earliest bookings was from a lady called Vicki Espin and her husband Neil. I gave them 10 per cent off for their double booking. I remember taking down their credit card details, putting the phone down and going straight over to the card machine and keying in £3,600. My bank manager had been on holiday and, when he returned, he phoned me and said, 'I think there's a problem with your account – it's £20,000 in the black!' 'Ah,' I replied, trying to sound cool. 'Things have taken off just a little in the last week!'

On Saturday, 16 October 1999, 27 people arrived at a country hotel near Coventry in the West Midlands to attend the first-ever coach-training session of the British Coaching Academy. Until then, these people had bought only a promise. Now we had to deliver. I had approached five experts on coaching and we put together a two-day course for these students to learn how to become personal coaches.

For those two days, I stood outside the hall biting my nails, absolutely terrified that people would hate it. As the students filed out at the end of the weekend I asked them to fill in feedback forms. Going through them, I discovered that the responses were amazingly positive. I suddenly thought, 'Oh, my God, we've got something here. This is going to be good.' I got a bit carried away and I booked another course the following month, which was attended by only eleven people. Then in December there were 35. From then on we never looked back.

The timing was perfect. There was an unsatisfied demand for coach training that many people had recognised but had never done anything about. About a year after we started we were informed in a letter that we could no longer use 'British' in our company name. I now know that the letter was instigated by a jealous competitor. This can often happen when you start a new business, so we changed the name to the Life Coaching Academy. Later we realised that the name was quite restrictive, since, by then, we were doing business and corporate coaching, so we decided to call it simply the Coaching Academy.

Five years after setting up, more than 5000 people have attended Coaching Academy courses and we have done over £12 million of business. Many customers are from overseas. They find out about us on the Internet. We also have many corporate clients including Vodaphone, Orange, BT, ICI, IBM and American Express, who send their staff, especially from their human-resources department, for training. Vicki Espin, who was a student on that very first course, is now director of coach development at the Coaching Academy. She and her husband Neil are two of Britain's top corporate coaches and they work with some of the biggest UK business names.

It's such a liberating feeling to be able to knock down your debts one at a time.

My personal nightmare was also over. I had already sold my flat, so I no longer had mortgage arrears but I also paid off my credit cards, then tackled the car problem. I still owed the HP company £10,000. I phoned them and asked, 'If I pay it off today what figure will you accept?' 'Seven thousand pounds if you pay it into our bank account by three o'clock,' came the reply. So I went straight to the bank and asked for £7,000 in cash, but they did not have that amount in the safe. So I had to go to another branch to get the cash and I paid it in just before the deadline. I've still got that paying-in slip. Then I phoned my girl-friend and said, 'I've done it. I've paid it off!' It's such a liberating feeling to be able to knock down your debts one at a time.

A chap who ran a training company who wanted to buy the *Achievement Report* company also approached me. I do not think there is such a thing as 'break-even'. Breaking even means you have lost. The sad fact is that the magazine was losing money. We did a deal for about £30,000 spread over twelve months, which was a big mistake. I should have got the money upfront. I ended up with only £7,000 because, as soon as he got his hands on the magazine, he started accusing me of breach of contract. I did not consider that I had broken any contract. He thought I had, so the payments stopped 'until we've sorted this out'. Sorry if I'm starting to sound like Alan Partridge but in the end I did have the last laugh. The new owners ran the magazine for three issues and then folded it because it didn't make them any money, either. They probably lost more than I ever did.

Getting rid of the magazine was a weight off my mind. The Coaching Academy was by now doing so well that I gave the £7,000 settlement cheque to my parents as a gift. After selling my flat, I tried to get a mortgage for another place but, because I had been in arrears in the past, the lenders wouldn't give me one, so I waited a while and paid £63,000 in cash for my next home. It was the most exciting, life-changing moment and things just haven't stopped improving since. It has been an incredible roller-coaster ride.

I'm not telling you all this in order to blow my own trumpet, just to explain how it can be a big struggle but, if you keep holding on to your self-belief, you can do it too when you sack your boss.

KEEPING COSTS DOWN

Bartering is a great way to keep down costs, especially in the early days.

As I mentioned earlier, if you have a skill such as writing or designing where your only expense is time, swap it for something you need that would normally cost you hard cash. Say you need to run some radio adverts to boost your public-relations business. You could go to the radio station and offer to publicise one of their events. If you have already had contact with some presenters, get them to put in a word for you and, if they agree, they could pay you in airtime.

Everyone wins. It costs you both nothing.

You could make the deal more complicated by swapping the airtime with a company that wants to advertise on radio and you get paid in something they sell, perhaps a vehicle. Bartercard is a great system that originated in Australia and is in use over here. Once you join you can barter for virtually anything. A client came on our training programme and 'paid' us 2,500 Bartercard pounds. I can go to the Bartercard directory and swap them for something we need, perhaps £2,500 worth of cardboard packaging, and, if I want 10,000 units, they might say, 'That will cost you 2,500 barter pounds.' You do the deal and write out a 'barter cheque'. I have now swapped my course for boxes, even though the man who came on the course did not sell boxes. It is a good system. Australians are also brilliant at franchising and licensing. The country is so big that if you want to open a shop in Melbourne and you live in Perth it is easier to franchise than it is to try to manage a shop thousands of miles away.

TIP

Quite often, one of the first clients in your business will be your previous employer. If you leave on amicable terms, you can sell your services back as a freelancer to the company you worked for. It's very tempting because you know the business and you have gained your first customer. But be very careful, or you could end up back in the same job, working for the boss you fired but without all the benefits, such as paid sick leave and holiday pay.

WHAT PRICE SHOULD I CHARGE?

You have sacked your boss; you have set up an office. Now you need to decide what to charge your customers.

You might be saying, 'Hang on, Jonathan, I haven't any customers yet.' I will come to that in a minute, but too many people starting out in business do not put enough thought into how much they are going to charge. *If you run a business it has to be profitable.*

Break-even equals loss. If your business is not profitable, then you cannot pay the people who are going to be closest to you throughout your life as an entrepreneur, the Inland Revenue and Customs and Excise. There is no escaping them. They like being paid, so you've got to pay them. You've got to pay yourself, too, and it's nice to have a bit of money left over for contingencies because things don't always go according to plan. Also, it's good to have a little bit of cash to spend on a weekend away or to go on holiday. When you are self-employed you need more holidays, not fewer, than when you worked for someone.

TIP

A little while ago, I discovered the hidden benefits of holidays. Even though you think they are a big expense, you get renewed enthusiasm and a new lease of life when you come home. Also, you will often get your best ideas on holiday. I can go away for just two days and come back absolutely buzzing, so it is definitely worth it. It happens because you are *out* of your working situation and can look at your business like an outsider looking in. On page 75, I will tell you about the dangers of working *in* your business, rather than *on* it.

You can lose business by undercharging. If someone does not charge enough, you immediately think he can't be much good (remember that 'accountant'). A conference-organising company once phoned me and said, 'We've never booked someone like you before but we have a client who wants to hire you for their conference. How much would you charge?' I asked a few questions including, 'Where is it?' 'The Grosvenor House in Park Lane, London,' came the reply.

'How many people?' I asked.

'Three hundred and they're senior consultants from around the country. They're staying for two days and we want you to open the second day.'

I then asked what figure they had in mind and I am ashamed to admit I was actually thinking in terms of about £600 to £700.

'Well, around about two,' was the reply.

'Two hun—'

'Two thousand.'

Thinking quickly and in true negotiating style, I said, 'Well, actually I was thinking of £2,500 but you'd better take that back to the client.'

All they had to do was sell a £500 difference, rather than the whole amount. I got the job for £2,500 and the client booked me again three months later.

So how much are *you* going to charge your customers? Do not charge the bare minimum. If you settle for the bare minimum that is all you are going to get. Each person's financial goals are different. When you are planning your goals, do not forget that, whenever you start up a business, your costs are going to be far greater than you expected and you are going to make far less than you planned. Every price is expensive until you have built up the value to justify that cost.

Say you were a hairdresser and you wanted to charge more, simply because if you charged £5 for a haircut you would never make a profit. You have got to build up the value of your product. The value can be increased by the salon's décor, the name, the logo and the fact that you offer complimentary teas and coffees. There is a big difference between going into a barber's shop, paying a fiver and being there for less than ten minutes and going to a beautiful salon, paying £50 and being there for over an hour. The more expensive salon is not offering just a hair-cutting service but an experience.

If you want to be profitable it is better to aim for the upper end of the market. We all know it is harder to ski uphill, just as it is harder to put your prices up.

One luxury hotel chain found a way to cut back on their furnishings bill. Each suite had several telephones in each room, one on either side of the bed, one in the bathroom and another on the desk. To save money the management took away all the phones except one. In these days when everyone has a mobile, it seemed to make sense. However, that one little difference changed the perceived value of the service. Immediately, the suite lost its five-star status and was listed as a 'standard' room. So if you want to be profitable it is better to aim for the upper end of the market. We all know it is harder to ski uphill, just as it is harder to put your prices up.

Too many businesses start too low. They think that by being cheap they will attract customers. If you price yourself cheaply you will get cheap customers. My friend David was just a few months older than I and, at the age of thirteen, he started performing as a magician and charged £5. Of course five quid when you are thirteen or fourteen is a lot of money for doing something you love. It just wasn't work.

We used to sit next to each other at school and I was constantly talking to him about how to learn magic tricks. There was a magic shop near our home town, Shanklin on the Isle of Wight. I used to go there on Saturdays to soak up the showbiz atmosphere, hoping someone famous might come in. It didn't happen very much on the Isle of Wight. I would buy tricks and go home to practise them, but I would never bother to read the instructions, so I wasn't very good. Eventually, I started doing kids' birthday parties as well, but I charged £7 – £2 more than David.

My first-ever show was for a Cub Scout group who booked me for a thirty-minute performance. My timing was so bad that, after twenty minutes, I was running out of tricks, but I survived. I realised it was too cheap, as there were about thirty or forty children there. I figured that it just wasn't adequate compensation for the effort I'd put in, so I put up prices, first to £10, then to £15. Then I worked out that, if I ran the whole two-hour party and included a games element, I could charge £45 to £50. That was when I made my first business opponent. David and I fell out big time because he and his mum thought I was charging too much but I was actually working more than he was and, for that reason, I was charging more as well. That is also when I realised that it is a myth that if you charge less you will get more work.

When they start businesses, people often say, 'We'll undercut everyone.' It can work for a while, but undercutting does not really have a long-term future unless you are going to sell in huge quantities, like Wal-Mart in the States or Asda in the UK. They can afford to sell on price because of the volumes they shift, but, if your quantities start reducing and customers begin to fall away, there is no way back from disaster. If you are a small company trying to undercut large concerns then your rivals will just cut their prices and, because of their size, they will simply drive you out of business.

TIP

When I was doing kids' birthday parties, I discovered that one of the downsides of turning your hobby into your business is that you forget it *is* a business and put every penny back into your hobby. You will never make any profit because you will always be ploughing money back into something that, after all, you love doing. If you are going to run your hobby as a business, there has to be a degree of mental separation between the two elements. I found that when I was doing magic shows, I was always spending my profits on buying tricks and books on magic, as well as going to magic conventions. I was earning a lot of money for someone so young but I could never understand where all the money went.

Don't make the mistake of swapping time for money. So many self-employed people get into a business where, if they don't turn up for work at nine o'clock in the morning, that business doesn't make any money. It is a mistake. I learned from experience that it is the wrong way to work.

When I was out in Ibiza working my hypnotism act in the hotels of Es Cana, I made the mistake of swapping time for money. I'd work for two hours in an evening for which I was paid £100. That would be it until the next day, when I'd do my two hours once more and get paid again. If I wasn't working I wasn't earning anything. I see so many people who are working as consultants or in the entertainment industry in particular, who don't seem to get out of the idea that, if they do break their leg, they can't work. I have a taxi driver friend and I phoned him to take me to the airport but he had hurt his foot and could not. In fact, he told me that he could not work for a week so could not make any money, which was terrible. What he could have done was subcontract his taxi out to someone else who could have driven it on his behalf, splitting the fare and giving him at least some income. Instead, he sat at home resting his injured foot and not earning anything.

There are two types of cash flow – negative cash flow and positive cash flow. Negative cash flow is money going away from you and positive cash flow is the funds that come to you. It's simple. The idea is to have more flowing towards you than away. It sounds obvious but many business owners will say, 'I need to spend to make money.' That's OK just as long as you do make money as well as spend it. Quite often, people do not expect to make a profit for a long time – and they don't. They think it is perfectly acceptable to keep paying out again and again without getting anything back. You have to make a profit as quickly as possible, otherwise you will become like the dotcom companies that spent millions of pounds of other people's money and never got any customers.

ACTION PLAN

Sit down and work out just how much you are going to charge for your goods or services. Look at what others charge but remember: cheap prices attract cheap customers.

CHAPTER 6

PROFESSIONALISM

Once you have sacked your boss, you become your company's biggest asset. You need an image to sell yourself and your company to potential customers.

YOUR IMAGE AND YOUR COMPANY'S IMAGE

Hire a good graphic designer to create a 'look' for your business but be prepared for that image to change over time as your company grows and evolves. How you start is not going to be how you finish. You don't need to go to an expensive design agency when there are thousands of graphic designers around the country who can do just as good a job and charge around £30 an hour. For four or five hours' work, you will get half a dozen logos to choose from and, *hey presto!*, you have an image for your new company. For another couple, you can have a template for your business cards, letterhead, compliment slips and even your website home page.

Once you have an image, don't be afraid to change it. The worst thing you can have is a dated image. More than a decade after London's phone numbers first changed, you still see business cards, letterheads, delivery vans and even shop windows with the old 01 code for London. Those companies have not updated their image, which says they are stuck in the past. Some people say that once you have a logo never change it. They are wrong. Look at big multinational corporations such as Shell. Over the decades their logo has been modified and updated to keep pace with changing styles. To change your image now and again is not a bad thing unless you do what the Post Office did. They changed their name to Consignia. People loved the name 'Post Office' and they had a full-scale revolt on their hands as a result. There was nothing wrong with 'Post Office' – it was simply a new marketing manager trying to make his mark. In the end, they went back to plain old 'Post Office'.

Every year, I look at the Coaching Academy's logo. I might think that perhaps the edges are a bit harsh and need softening to make the company's image look friendlier, or I might decide to change the print colour. It is easy to do and doesn't cost much, but it gives the impression that the company is evolving to keep pace with the times.

You don't get a second chance to make a first impression. Researchers claim that people make up their minds about you within the first five seconds of meeting. It may be true but don't let it panic you because we do get second chances. Nobody is going to judge you in five seconds and never speak to you again.

Dress like the person you want to be. If you want to be rich and successful then dress like someone who *is* rich and a success. People with a big ego fall into the trap of dressing down because they think they don't need to try. Leave dressing down to Woody Allen. He can get away with wearing a dinner jacket and trainers. He's allowed to do that. You are not. If you are appearing in front of an audience, be better dressed than they are. It doesn't mean you have to spend thousands of pounds on an outfit, but make sure you dress with style. If you are a man, rely on a female partner or friend to advise you. Most men, including myself, haven't got a clue.

SOME TIPS ABOUT YOUR BUSINESS CARD

- Don't create something that's so beautiful and expensive that you don't want to give them out freely.

- The average thickness of business cards is 385 gsm.

- Contact local printers and get recommendations from friends who have used them.

▓ Avoid the 'print your own' machines in shopping centres and railway stations. They don't look professional.

▓ Expect to pay £80–100 for 500 cards printed in one colour (if you supply artwork, expect to pay more for design).

▓ Put all your contact details on the card – telephone, email, fax, mobile and address.

▓ Put a reminder of what you do on the card, for example: John Smith, Professional & Personal Performance Coach.

▓ You may find that your card will work better for you if you opt for putting your mission statement or the offer of a 'free introductory offer' on the reverse.

PROFESSIONAL STATIONERY

This can be used to send letters, invoices, contracts and any other correspondence and it is usually printed on 100 gsm paper. Printers should charge between £60 and £85 to print 500 one-colour letterheads from your camera-ready artwork. Never print your stationery on your inkjet printer: it will always look amateurish.

COMPLIMENT SLIPS

These are not essential but useful to include when sending things out to clients. You could, for example, attach them, with a brief, handwritten note on them, to something you are sending a client when a letter is not called for. Expect to pay a similar amount to what you would pay for headed paper.

ACTION PLAN

Use the space below to design your own business card. Keep it simple, a standard size and easy to read. Find other cards that you have been given, choose the designs that really appeal to you and copy them.

BUSINESS PREMISES

People judge you by the company that you keep – and that includes your business premises.

When I ran my magazine, I rented rooms in a draughty run down Victorian building. It was a health-and-safety nightmare with wires running everywhere. Our neighbours had a variety of absolutely amazing businesses, some involving the craziest ideas, while others were downright dodgy. One guy down the corridor was never in his office and official-looking people were always knocking on the door wanting to have a chat with him. It was almost embarrassing to say you had an office in that building.

Unfortunately, respectable businesses will become tarred with the same brush when you work from a building with a suspect reputation. Very quickly, we moved to a more respectable, council-run business centre elsewhere in Portsmouth. However, when I started the Coaching Academy, I used a London address, 17 Bedford Square. It was far more prestigious and projected an image of success and stability, and the post was forwarded to Portsmouth from there.

Nowadays, people are not interested where a business is based. It depends whether clients need to come to your premises. In fact, the advent of the Internet made it possible for many businesses to locate at the most remote addresses. It just depends on the kind of business you are in. If you are going to be in advertising, you must have a good address.

An image of success and stability is really important. So how do you create it? It can be done partly through self-belief and partly by constantly speaking to people. You can do it with your business name or even by the way you answer the telephone. Creating the impression that you are not fly-by-night and intend to be in business for quite a while can be tough on a tight budget.

So fake it till you make it. If you work from home to save on office rent, you can say to your clients, 'I'm very lucky I can work from home.' You would be amazed just how many people working for big companies will envy you for not having to commute and an entrepreneur may have built up their company from nothing only to have to cope with a large staff and the accompanying headaches. They might wish they worked from home with just one employee. (On page 159, I will explain the exit strategy – what to do when your business becomes too big.)

WHAT EQUIPMENT DO I NEED?

It's a question I am always being asked. If you are starting a manufacturing company that needs £1 million pounds worth of machinery and a hundred staff, then this is not the book for you. Most people who sack their boss will be starting a business on a budget, although I am sure some starting out with the help of this book will go on to run big businesses.

If you are starting a small business from home, the best thing you can go out and buy is a good suit and invest in some personal grooming so you will create a great impression when you meet people. You also need a personality and a fantastic attitude. Here's the good news, they cost nothing at all. You've got to get out there and meet people, so set up two, three or four appointments a day if you can. Start meeting people you have identified to help you reach your goal – you will be amazed at the doors that open if you keep trying. It is a small world and you will talk to people who know someone who can help you. The bigger and more supportive your network, the greater your chances of success.

You do not need expensive equipment to start your business. You need yourself. In the early days, *you* are the business. You need to invest in yourself rather than an expensive computer.

CHAPTER 7

PLANNING

'One thing most companies lack is clarity. They don't know exactly what they're doing and where they're going. If companies had clarity of focus they would be far more successful.'

Vicki Espin, executive coach

YOUR BUSINESS PLAN

Ask most people what their goals are in life and they will reply, 'Oh, I don't know.' Lottery winners often squander their jackpot quickly because they weren't expecting to win. They didn't have a plan. With no plan, what would you do with all the millions that suddenly appeared in your bank account? Why, spend it all, of course. You would buy things you didn't want or need because you never could. Unknown friends and relatives would come out of the woodwork and, before you realised it, there would be no money left. So having a plan is absolutely essential for anything, but especially for your new business.

 **Having a plan is absolutely essential for anything, but especially for your new business.**

Whatever business you go into, you will need a bank account, and with a bank account comes a bank manager. Your bank manager, and certainly his bosses, will want to see a business plan. Don't be fooled by the fancy forms the bank will give you – a business plan is a list of goals and a plan of action to achieve them. We spoke about these goals on page 12. Your plan needs to be a list of just ten things setting out exactly what you will do as your new venture grows. Number One is where you are now and Number Ten is where you want to be. Actually, I do it backwards. I start with the end result and work back to the starting point, listing the things I need to do to get where I want to be. That, to me, is a business plan but your bank won't accept it.

They will want to see the figures. The bank's business plan will tell them how many items you are going to sell, how many customers you will have and how much profit you are going to make. The truth is, you don't know, but it is a game you have to play.

When you have sacked your boss, getting the right bank manager will be vital to the success of your new venture. I had a terrible manager and, if I had stayed with that bank, I would probably not be writing this now. That's how vital it is. I read somewhere that you should interview bank managers when you are changing banks so, when I decided I had to switch from Barclays to another bank to save my business, I phoned up four banks. Three said, 'Come in and see us' but the fourth one said, 'I'll come and see you.' It was a life-changing moment when the man from Lloyds walked through my office door. As we were chatting, I asked, 'Have you ever run your own business?' 'No,' he said, 'but I've been involved with so many businesses that it feels as though I have.' Then he asked, 'What do you want?' to which I replied, 'I want a £5,000 overdraft facility.'

Seven years later, he is still my bank manager. As my business grew, he told me that I would be approached to move my accounts to a corporate manager but I chose to stay with him. I can phone him on his mobile at any time and ask him to switch money or sort out a payment for me and he will do it. It's a wonderful relationship that took time and trust to build, but he's a great guy. I remember that first meeting distinctly, as you always remember the moments that are crucial to everything – good and bad. For me it was a real defining moment and he probably didn't realise just how important that was. You never let on that you are desperate, because desperate people never get loans unless they pay over the odds with huge amounts of interest – and that's bad practice.

Don't ignore the plan. Once you have got the bank on side, don't throw away your plan. Stick your company goals on your mirror, where you can see them every morning.

You will find that, as an entrepreneur, you sleep less and get up earlier. As Paul McKenna once said to me, 'Every morning I get out of bed and think, "What can I do today to move me closer to my goal?" ' Failing to plan is planning to fail. I used to ignore advice like this but I have now learned that only by planning will you get a jump on the opposition, who may react only to the day-to-day ups and downs of business life.

ACTION PLAN

Use the next page to draw up your business plan. You do not need to include lots of sums and figures at this stage. Simply list the things you need to do to get the business going and then to develop the business for the first year. Set out what you want to do and a timescale with a date by which you want to achieve that part of your plan. Make that list now. Then keep it and fill out the date when you complete each task.

Requirements	Planned date	Completion date

FIVE-YEAR PLAN

If you have the entrepreneurial spirit, you will never retire because you love what you do. You cannot possibly conceive of a time when you will get out of bed in the morning and have nothing to aim for. At the time of writing, I am 34 years old and I already have the next five years planned out. I know exactly how I want to grow my coaching business, improve it and add more elements to the company. You should have a five-year plan, too.

Often we overestimate the amount we can achieve in a year, but underestimate just how much progress can be made in five. My five-year plan currently includes a goal of opening a coaching school in America, the biggest market in the world. I also aim to add a European flavour so that we are not just a British company but a European one as well. If you have a great product it doesn't really matter in which country it originates. We are quite happy to drive German cars and buy Japanese television sets, and international boundaries aren't really a problem. It will be a major challenge for us because we would become the largest coaching organisation in the world. It would be a lot of fun and to succeed would give everyone in the company a real sense of achievement.

Even when you have achieved something very positive you will never be able to sit back and think, 'That's it, I don't need to do any more' because there is always more to be done. A business is an ongoing process. It may be perfect for about five or ten minutes and then something will happen. It is like constantly juggling to keep all the balls in the air – in a howling gale. You have to enjoy change because everything is changing constantly.

I am amazed when I go into companies. They are often family businesses, which is like walking into a time warp. Nothing has changed for thirty or forty years. These people just don't keep up with the times, and they have to. It's almost as though they are in the business for their own benefit rather than their customers'. I see businesses like this and think 'Why do you exist?' They exist purely to give themselves a job. Rather than work for someone else, they provide themselves with employment. To me that is not really a business.

TIME MANAGEMENT

The downside of the entrepreneur's character is that they get a bit too involved. One minute they are buzzing round the office changing light bulbs, the next they will be signing huge cheques before they are off to a meeting where they will tell people with far more knowledge how to do their jobs.

You will want to be involved in every aspect of your business. After all, it is your company and you love it. Because you love it, you will, if you are not careful, devote every hour of the day to making sure it is a success. As an entrepreneur you need to know your strengths and weaknesses. You must also stay focused on your goals and remember the outcome you want, which means you have to manage your time properly. Work hard by all means, but work smart, too. Do not waste time on things that won't make you money or will deflect you from your plan.

EMAIL AND PHONE CALLS

Email is a wonderful thing but let's be honest: how much time do you waste checking your emails? Do you interrupt what you are doing every five or ten minutes to see if you have any messages? If you do, your day is run by dancing to someone else's tune. Time really is money when you are self-employed, so why not discipline yourself to check your email just twice a day?

It is the same with phone calls, though I am as guilty as anyone. Having your mobile switched on all the time is not the best way to manage your time, either. You cannot concentrate on anything. Turn off your mobile and record a message on it asking callers to leave a message, letting them know that you will be checking the messages every hour and you will get back to them today. That way you control whom you speak to and when. If you don't prioritise your day, you end up doing only urgent things rather than the important things that could be making you money.

EAT THAT FROG

The best advice on managing your life and prioritising your day comes from Brian Tracy, who has written a book called *Eat That Frog*. He says that, surely, the worst thing you can do in any day is eat a frog. So, if you have to eat a frog, why not get it over with early and tuck into it at the start of the day? That way you've got it out of the way and the rest of the day is clear. The frog, of course, is the thing you hate doing, the job you can't stand and have been putting off for ages. Don't think of your frog as a huge monster, but imagine eating it a slice at a time. You can tackle your particular frog in stages. Just don't put off doing it. If you have two frogs to eat on a particular day, eat the uglier one first.

PAPERWORK

Paperwork has always been the bane of my life. I hate it and you may, too, but it will always be there, so tackle it.

Even with email there is always going to be paperwork. If you have the technology, and it isn't expensive, I would suggest setting up a system whereby you handle a piece of paper only once. If it needs to be kept, it is scanned and archived on your PC; if not, throw it away.

I hear people saying, 'I'm drowning in paperwork.' If it is all filed away neatly, daily, you won't drown. If you can't tackle it get someone to do it for you. You could also take a tip from Richard Branson, who carries a notepad everywhere and jots down everything he needs to do. It helps you focus on what needs doing now. That way, you don't spend half the day hunting for things and being distracted from the essentials.

ACTION PLAN

Use the rest of this page to write down your own strengths and weaknesses when it comes to time management. Be honest. If you know you fritter away time reading emails when you could be making sales, list it as a weakness and work on making yourself more disciplined.

Strengths	Weaknesses

WORKING *ON* THE BUSINESS, NOT *IN* IT

In a book called *The E-Myth* (meaning the entrepreneurial myth), American Michael Gerber wrote that the baker who makes fantastic bread is the last person who should set up a business selling his own produce.

If you are so much in love with your product, you won't be able to see the wood for the trees. There's a big difference between being *in love* with your product and *loving* it. If you are in love with your business no one can do it as well as you and you have to do everything. In fact, if the baker took someone on, he'd be watching him or her like a hawk instead of concentrating on running the concern, which means it can never grow. It will always be limited by the baker's time.

The best person to run a bakery is an entrepreneur who does not know a great deal about baking bread but can hire bakers to make the best. Although they love the business they are not so *in love* with it that they strive for perfection and never make a profit. The customer doesn't care as long as the bread is fresh and sold at the right price.

You need to be able to take a 'helicopter' view to manage effectively. If you are *in* the business, rather than *on* it, you can never see its challenges or its opportunities because you are so involved in ordering the paperclips, changing the light bulbs and sweeping the floor that you take your eye off the important things, such as working out a sales and marketing strategy and chasing debtors. It is very easy to do.

Quite often, I have flashes of inspiration after I've been away on holiday or away from the office for a few days. Sometimes, all it takes is a walk. When you are away from the hubbub of phones ringing and people asking you questions, you can start working on the business. Sometimes, you need to go away to work effectively. Just by taking a Friday afternoon off and going away for a long weekend, you can give yourself a whole new lease of life. If you are there at work every single day, you stop seeing what is obvious to everyone else around you.

It's exactly the same with relationships. You may think you are revealing something to your best friend by saying, 'Things haven't been right recently.' And, when he replies, 'Everyone knows that,' you are stunned. You are so involved in it you think no one else knows. That's where a coach is so useful. They can come in, look at your ideas and help you explore options and possibilities that you might never have considered yourself. Many people go through life thinking they have no choices and coaching allows people to realise that this is not the case. Coaches can look at all the options objectively and decide which one is the most appropriate to move clients to where they want to be. Without that element of choice people get stuck in a rut.

Ruts and coffins are very similar. Both inhibit new development, impede progress and leave you feeling bad.

TECHNICAL STUFF

Here is some technical information that you will need to set up your company. Store this information away, then we can get on with the most important task for any business – finding customers.

TRADING STATUS

You can choose whether to begin business as a *sole trader*, to set up a *partnership* with another professional or to establish your business as a *limited company*. All the options have tax and legal obligations, so you should consult a qualified accountant to advise you on the best option to suit your particular circumstances.

VAT REGISTRATION

Whether you trade as a sole trader, partnership or limited company, you do not have to register for VAT until your turnover reaches a minimum level (currently £60,000 per annum). You may, however, wish to register for VAT before this. Some professionals working with corporate clients believe that they must be VAT-registered in order to appear successful. VAT registration has some benefits: for example, you can claim VAT back on items bought for your business, or, if you are a sole trader, it forces you into the good discipline of doing your accounts every quarter rather than leaving them until the end of the year. Again, you should consult a qualified accountant to advise you in your own circumstances.

TAX AND NATIONAL INSURANCE

However you choose to trade, you must advise the Inland Revenue about your new business earnings. You may need to pay income tax on any earnings you make as a sole trader. The Inland Revenue will probably ask you to complete a self-assessment tax return at the end of the financial year. The rules for directors of limited companies are different. They often pay themselves using dividends, which can be more tax-efficient, but this has implications for National Insurance payments, which may affect future state pension rights. Again, consult a qualified accountant to advise you on your own circumstances.

BANK ACCOUNTS

Limited companies must have their own bank account. As a sole trader you may use your own bank account, but it would be much simpler to set up a separate one for your new venture. If you run your business account and personal account separately you won't have to spend extra time splitting your business and personal finances when you come to complete your tax return at the end of each financial year. This will also save you money if you pay an accountant to do the job for you. It's also a good idea to save some money earned from your business activities to pay for tax, unexpected expenses and marketing activities to promote your business further.

DATA PROTECTION

People worry about the Data Protection Act far more than is necessary. Anyone storing data that can identify an individual should investigate whether they should register. This data includes names and addresses, email addresses and account details. The registration fee is £35 per year and registration can be organised by calling 01625 545745 or logging onto http://www.dataprotection.gov.uk.

Note that the information supplied above is not advice but for guidance and to highlight areas that you should consider when setting up your business. It is important that you consult a qualified professional, who will ensure that you do it correctly.

ACTION PLAN

Contact your bank to set up a separate account for your new business. If you think being VAT-registered at this stage would help you or if you are likely to turn over in excess of £60,000, you need to contact Customs and Excise for a VAT number.

"RUNNING YOUR BUSINESS"

CHAPTER 8

A CRASH COURSE IN MARKETING

If you do not have any customers, you do not have a business – you have only a dream. To turn your dream into reality, you must let people know that you exist. That's marketing.

'Marketing' is what happens to get the phone ringing. 'Sales' is what happens once the phone rings. Marketing uses a series of techniques to heighten awareness of you and your business and to stimulate the public's desire to find out more. In marketing jargon, this is sometimes termed turning a 'suspect' into a 'prospect'.

The next chapter is all about selling, which is the stage where you convert a prospect into a client, but there is a crossover, because, while you are marketing, you are also selling. If you answer the phone in a professional manner, then you are selling your company to a potential customer at what may be their first point of contact. People no longer buy a product just for a service: they are actually buying into the company. Marketing was one thing the Coaching Academy did very well right from the start. If you get the sales and marketing right everything else falls into place, and we got it right. It all seemed like common sense but nobody else in the world we operated in was doing it. As a result, we became very good at generating new business.

People still come to me and say they don't know how to get customers. Getting customers is the easy part. We advertised widely and sent out lots of direct mail. I also built relationships with other companies. If you have strategic relationships with other companies then it makes life a lot easier and you don't have to do it all by yourself. We gobbled up the market share very, very quickly. You need someone to spur you on in business. The American company was keeping me on my toes. It had already trained about 350 coaches. That was my target. When I broke the hundred-coaches-trained barrier, there was a moment of celebration then suddenly, before we knew it, we had reached 1,000. Our rival has never grown at all.

You must research your market constantly to find out what has worked and what has not. I always ask my customers: How did you find out about us? Why did you choose us? No one has ever said it is because we are the cheapest. We are not. The answer I hear the most, and the one that makes me the happiest, is, 'You seem the most professional.' As I explained when we were discussing what to charge your customers, people will pay extra for professionalism. We don't mind paying 10 per cent extra for good service in a restaurant and we would rather go into a hotel where we are greeted with respect and treated as a valued guest than be somebody who is just occupying a room for the night. It is the same with businesses.

HOW TO FIND CUSTOMERS

I am going to explain the Sixteen Pillars of Marketing. I call them 'pillars of marketing' because you should never build your business on just one method of driving customers through your door. Too many businesses balance their whole livelihood very precariously on only one way of generating business income. You must build your business on lots of different strategies so that, if one goes wrong, you have others to fall back on. So, if one strategy doesn't work so well for a few weeks or months, it doesn't matter because you've got some other means of bringing in the business.

I have seen new businesses blow several thousand pounds, their entire budget, on a half-page advertisement in the *Daily Mail*. I know 3 million people are going to see it, but it is unlikely to make the business explode overnight. Others have spent a fortune on a website hoping for instant success. It does not happen.

One man I know held a seminar in the UK and relied on direct mail to advertise it. He spent all his money on the mailshot and did not sell a single ticket because the Royal Mail workers went on strike. You need to try a little bit of everything and build on the parts that work.

One of the most effective business tools, which I believe will become even more important in the future, is networking. You will be meeting and getting to know people who can help your business develop. You can hide behind your website but it's not exactly satisfying. Marketing your business can be great fun.

The Sixteen Pillars are the most powerful, yet surprisingly simple, marketing tools that have proved to grow a business like yours. Follow these suggestions and you will be successful. None is expensive and some are free. They are simple to apply.

1. DEVELOPING YOUR CLIENT LIST

Making use of contacts you already have is the quickest way of finding customers.

Many people, when starting a new business, go out looking for customers among people they don't know, completely forgetting that they already know lots of people. Don't do it the hard way. Do it the easy way. Think about who you know. Contact previous employers and work colleagues, friends of friends, other business people you deal with regularly and so on. Also, think about clients *they* know and work with. This is all marketing, and it is all totally free.

Do you belong to any professional associations, unions or organisations outside your line of business? If you are now or have ever been a member, why not take an active role? You will be amazed at how soon you can become that organisation's expert on your speciality with opportunities to promote your business in the pages of their magazine, journal or at regional meetings. Don't forget the networking opportunities of Chambers of Commerce as well. Make a list of all the different types of people you know under the following headings. I'm sure you can think of others too:

- friends

- brothers and sisters

- cousins

- parents or step-parents

- grandparents

- in-laws

- aunts and uncles

- godparents

- neighbours

- colleagues

- clients

- suppliers

- gym/golf/tennis partners

- club members

Then, for each of these categories, add their friends and relatives – for example, your brother-in-law's folks, his colleagues, golf partners and friends.

Then you can write down all the names of people you know under these headings and, before you know it, you will quickly have built up a database of potential clients who already know of you. Some of these potential clients you will be happy to contact directly; with others, you may want to ask your shared contact to make the introduction. Whether you do this by telephone or letter is up to you.

ACTION PLAN

Use the rest of this page to draw up a list of contacts you already know who could become potential customers. You should be able to come up with at least thirty names on your list.

2. NETWORKING

Don't be a hermit! Get yourself known.

When marketing your business, networking has nothing to do with 'network marketing', which is totally different. Networking is all about getting you and your company known. The more relationships you have, the more business you will do.

Many entrepreneurs find their clients through personal contacts and networking, which means talking to people. You must be able to explain clearly what your business is and you must be able to do this well, or your contact may misunderstand you. What you need is an 'elevator speech'. This is a simple explanation about your business and its potential benefit. It should last no longer than twenty seconds and its name comes from the fact that lift manufacturers have found that, typically, you will wait twenty seconds for an elevator, or lift, and the journey will probably last that length of time. Those twenty seconds are usually occupied with examining your nails, staring at your shoes and watching the indicator light. Basically, you do everything you can to avoid conversation with the other human beings occupying the same three or four square feet with you. So, here is a wonderful opportunity to network, but you have to get your point across very, very quickly indeed. If someone asks you what you do while you are both waiting for or riding in a lift, you will have just twenty seconds to deliver an informative and exciting description.

Create and practise your own elevator speech. It will not be time wasted because you will need to talk about your new venture wherever you go. Avoid giving your potential clients a hard sell, but just remind them who you are, what you do and enquire whether you can help them. An important aspect of personal contact is your own image. Take a good look at yourself and the way that you stand and speak. Make sure that you have an easy and nonconfrontational manner so people feel comfortable in your company. If they are not at ease, they won't become your client or customer. Remember, you are a professional, so dress, act and speak like one.

The number-one tool of the professional networker is the business card; and the second most important thing is to make sure you have them on you!

The number-one tool of the professional networker is the business card; and the second most important thing is to make sure you have them on you! How often have you met someone who says, 'I've got a card but I don't have it on me'? When you go out in the morning you pick up your money and your keys, so make sure you take your business cards too. Become an avid business card collector. Exchanging cards is a useful way of breaking the ice and opens up opportunities for you to tell each other what you do. In the travel industry when someone meets and shakes hands with anyone, they always have their card ready in the other hand.

You may have noticed that people go one of two ways when offering business cards. There are those who are incredibly proud of theirs because they have spent a lot of money on them. They take one out and show you how it is made from a shiny, indestructible laminate and it won't tear, saying something like, 'Look, it's got my photograph as well as a hologram of me. If you just tilt it to the right you can see me winking at you.' You might say, 'That's very clever, can I have one?' to which they reply 'Oh no, they're far too expensive to give away!' Then they put them away in a box.

Then there are those who find themselves at a railway station and spend a couple of quid and couple of minutes tapping out a business card on the machine at the end of Platform 5. Out pop a handful of cards printed on high-quality toilet paper, which gives them a tacky grey tinge. I knew a businessman who did just that and, because he was in a bit of a hurry, missed off a very important piece of information – his name! Make sure you put your name on your cards along with a contact phone number, your street address and email address. Do not put a long list of letters after your name thinking it will impress. Most people don't really care whether you've got an O-level in biology or a PhD. If you have a website, include it on the card because anyone interested in your business will check out your website to find out more about you.

You also need a logo. Do not do the design yourself unless you are a graphic designer and certainly do not use clip art from your computer. Look in Yellow Pages or on www.yell.com and check out some graphic designers. Better still, find a logo you like and find out who designed it. Ask for some roughs or sample logos from previous clients, which means that you don't pay them and they have to impress you. Make sure you use your card to explain your line of business by including your slogan or a strapline to sum up, in a handful of words, exactly what you do. You can even use the back of the card to make an introductory offer on your product.

Do not go out and buy 5,000 business cards just because it is the cheapest option. You will not be saving money. A few hundred will do, because I can guarantee that, within a few months of starting up, you will be chucking out the old ones and updating them with new information, your new image and a new strapline, because your business will have evolved.

How do you judge the effectiveness of a networking event? It's definitely not by the number of cards you give out. Networking is really about how many business cards you collect. If you only give out your cards you have to keep your fingers crossed that the people you met will contact you. By being proactive and collecting cards, you will be gathering information about potential customers. The situation is now under your control and *you* can contact *them* so make sure that those precious cards do not languish in a drawer.

 Avoid the hard sell – just let the potential client know who you are and that you are there, in case they are interested in doing business.

Within a week of receiving a new business card, you can follow up with a telephone call to say how much you enjoyed meeting them at whatever venue or event it was. Avoid the hard sell – just let the potential client know who you are and that you are there, in case they are interested in doing business.

If you don't do this, the chances are that, if you have given someone your business card in the hope that they keep their promise to ring you, they won't. In the week since you met, a lot of things will have happened to them and they have far more important things to think about than you. However, if you have been proactive, it doesn't matter because you can take control of the situation and follow up on the initial contact.

Recently, I met a man who regularly went to networking events and collected fifty business cards at a time. That meant he met, spoke to and interacted with fifty people in an evening. He did that a couple of times a week, forty-eight weeks of the year. Unless you are like that person who is obviously a born networker, it can be slightly daunting to walk into a room full of strangers and, in the words of that cheesy phrase, 'turn strangers into friends and friends into customers'.

When you enter a room full of people you don't know, I want you to imagine that you are there to win a prize. The prize is a successful business, with lots and lots of clients or customers. But what do you do if you get caught with someone who is boring you senseless and you feel as though you just can't get away? You need to make sure you are polite and make your excuses before moving on to meet someone new. You never know, 'the bore' might turn out to be one of your best customers one day.

Because you have been meeting so many people, you will come across some you feel you can introduce to others and, by doing this, you will be contributing to the networking process. You might say, 'Vanessa, you're looking for a printer for your business card. Well, I've just been talking to John over here. John, come and meet Vanessa. You do business cards at your printing company, don't you?' You will be running around the room all evening making connections for other people and, at the end of the evening, it could well be you standing at the door shaking people's hands and thanking them for coming! You will have a pocket full of business cards and everyone there will think it's your party.

ACTION PLAN

Use this page to write out your elevator speech. We speak at around 180 words a minute, so a twenty-second speech needs to be no more than sixty words. It must grab attention at the outset, so do not ramble or bore, and it must give the listener a chance to contact you. Use a tape recorder to practise and time it to make sure you stay focused.

TIP

Remember: a business card has two sides. Once you have chosen a design that pleases you, check the copy for accuracy. As soon as the shops open, visit the local printers in your area and get some quotes and samples of their work. The more you order at one time, the cheaper the cost per card. Think of 500 as a minimum quantity, then give them away freely. Don't forget, they cannot and will not work for you if you leave them in that cute little box that they are delivered in – or, worse, in your desk drawer.

3. JOIN A PROFESSIONAL ORGANISATION

Be a dedicated joiner of professional organisations, clubs, societies and associations.

As a newcomer, you may well be invited to address a meeting to introduce yourself and your business. What a golden opportunity. It is just too good to miss. You will make valuable new contacts for your personal network but look upon these as a fringe benefit. As with so much in life, you have to be seen to give before you can reasonably expect to receive. Business Network International (BNI) is a great organisation to join in order to build a wonderful network of people who are also there to meet other professionals. When you go to these events, remember that the second part of the word 'network' is 'work'. You are not there to have a beer with Jim at the bar because you haven't seen each other for a while. You are there to work, to build connections and establish a network of people who can help you achieve your goal. Always make sure you leave knowing more people than when you arrived.

ACTION PLAN

List five professional organisations you could join:

1. _____

2. _____

3. _____

4. _____

5. _____

_____

4. PUBLIC RELATIONS

Public relations is the cheapest way to get you and your company known to a much wider audience through media coverage.

Public relations, or PR, is absolutely crucial because it can cost you nothing, yet exposure in radio, television and the press gives you so much credibility. The easiest medium to get into is your local newspaper. Try telephoning the paper and ask for the business editor, to tell them about your business; or, if there is an interesting story attached to how you came to sack your boss, then contact the features editor. If you are lucky, they may even interview you over the telephone there and then. The key is to give them a story with a news angle and, if you can think of other local angles, so much the better.

As of now you have a topical story, anyway, but you may not realise it. Here's the story. You have just read a book called *Sack Your Boss!* by entrepreneur Jonathan Jay. It transformed your life because you did just that. You joined the growing army of workers who sacked their boss, hired themselves and started their own company. Try it. You never know, they might jump at it!

Even easier than the local paper is your free newspaper. 'Does anyone read the local freebie?' you may ask. They probably do, since it gives information about local events and sales, but, in any case, it doesn't matter, because you are mentioned in the paper. You can say to a potential client, 'Oh, did you read about me in the press recently?' You can photocopy the article and send it out as part of your promotional pack. People believe what they read in the papers. Your story is the real thing. Readers, listeners and viewers are not daft. They recognise that 'editorial' has earned its publication on merit as opposed to a paid-for advertisement, which many will disregard or disbelieve. They will even see your published or broadcast item as an implied endorsement by the editor. This is the next best thing to first-hand, word-of-mouth recommendation.

Think of the advertising that you could buy. A hundred pounds may fund a single entry of an eighth-page classified advertisement in a small-circulation magazine. A whole page can cost at least £2,000 and,

Your press release can gain you at least as much coverage as an advert – often more – and it will cost you zero, zilch, nada, nothing!

in national newspapers and magazines, it can cost more than £10,000. Your press release can gain you at least as much coverage as an advert – often more – and it will cost you zero, zilch, nada, nothing! What is more, it will be more credible as news.

If you phone the newspaper to tell them about your new venture and they express an interest but say, 'Send me a press release,' what do you do? A press release is simply a story about yourself and your company that you mail out to the editors of newspapers, radio or television stations. How do you write a press release? Well, if you go to a PR company and spend several hundred pounds, they will write you a lovely press release – but you can do it yourself. No one knows more about your company than you.

Your first press release should be about how you gave up work to follow your dream and set up your company. Tell them about your business, then follow it up with news angles, such as a major new client (ask the client's permission first), an anniversary, a new project or a new qualification. It's important to give them something that will grab their attention and interest their public. The next step is to be prepared when they call you back to ask for more information or to fix an interview.

A bad press release is worse than none at all. It will simply not be used.

If it is just an advertisement for your services, it will achieve only one thing: a telephone call inviting you to buy advertising. A well-crafted press release can be the best 'free' advertisement of all. One graduate from the Coaching Academy who sacked his boss and set up as a personal coach sent a press release to his local paper. A reporter telephoned and arranged to visit the house with a photographer. The interview appeared as a double-page spread across the centre pages of the business section.

The local radio station manager then read the interview and contacted the coach. The coach asked for and was granted permission to tape his subsequent discussion with the presenter and now uses that tape to send to potential clients as promotion for his services and confirmation of his credibility. The broadcast was heard by an executive at a local company, who invited the coach to do a presentation to his staff and paid him for the work he did. His only initial outlay had been a simple press release and a first-class stamp.

If your website is also featured, readers can learn more about you before they telephone. This turns them from the 'lukewarm leads' who have read your article into 'very warm leads' who have visited your site.

National newspapers and magazines can be more difficult to get into, but by no means impossible. It takes persistence, patience and professionalism. For optimum benefit, you need your contact details included in any article, and the way to encourage them to feature this is to develop an exclusive 'reader offer' or give the paper or magazine an exclusive article. A story in the national press, with your telephone number included, can have your phone ringing off the hook with sales and a full appointments diary within 24 hours. If your website is also featured, readers can learn more about you before they telephone. This turns them from the 'lukewarm leads' who have read your article into 'very warm leads' who have visited your site. You have grabbed their attention and the rest is up to you.

Whenever you have had something printed about you or your company, make lots of good-quality photocopies at your local print shop and send them out with your promotional material (not with your press release, since that is just for the press). Keep the originals, along with the masthead of the paper or cover of the magazine, in a portfolio that you can show people with pride. A book containing clear plastic pockets will display the pages well without breaking the bank and you can always splash out and frame the exceptional articles to put up on the office wall.

When you do visit your local TV or radio station and the interview goes well, make sure they know you are available to comment on your particular speciality. That way, if a relevant story breaks, they will call you and it will give you a chance to plug your business again. You might even get a regular slot. Many of the coaches who trained at the Coaching Academy now do regular phone-in spots at their local radio stations. Most newspaper editors also maintain a list of contacts and you could be on it.

If you are able to develop a working relationship with an editor, you can save a lot of cold calling by using this as the introduction to actually writing an article or series of articles in the paper or magazine. The article about an aspect of your practice will have all the benefits of a press release and you should be paid for it too.

 Your 'stake' is a few hours of your free time ... Your 'winnings' could be worth £10,000 in equivalent advertising or more.

There is a downside to PR. Publication of a paid advertisement is usually guaranteed but publication of your interview or feature is a gamble. It is, however, one of the few gambles worth taking, because your 'stake' is a few hours of your free time, a few sheets of paper, a handful of stamps, some envelopes and a couple of clicks of your mouse. Your 'winnings' could be £10,000 in equivalent advertising or more.

No public-relations firm on this planet can ever promise that your press release will be published or that it will definitely result in an interview or feature. If they do, they are lying! You do not want to do business with them. There are tricks of the trade that can take years of trial and error to learn. Some of the most useful are revealed in these pages so that you can use them immediately. Plenty of people have made these mistakes, but you don't have to.

Timing is vital. If you send your press release to the local paper and expect to see your practice featured in the next issue, you may, and probably will, be disappointed! Even daily papers, both local and national, often prepare feature articles several weeks in advance of publication.

Here is a rough guide to getting published. You should keep these timescales in mind when you are putting out a time-sensitive press release.

- For inclusion in TV documentaries, you may wait a year or more before your programme is screened. TV chat shows have a shorter lead time. Radio programmes offer the quickest coverage, especially local radio.

- Send your press release by first-class post and, just to drive the point home, write 'First Class' on the envelope (or use a preprinted first-class sticker). Better still, send it by email.

- Editors are always busy. They tend not to like Monday morning mail, since many have production meetings that day. They like to 'run down' on Fridays, so time your posting to arrive on Tuesday, Wednesday or Thursday.

- Have a clear idea about whom you want to reach through the press. If your objective is to attract local clients, there is no point in seeking national coverage, so focus on local publications and broadcasters.

- If you are seeking sales, fame and glory on a national scale, then aim for national press and broadcasting.

Now refine your target further.

- Identify your prime time target audience by sex, occupation, ethnic group, family status, economic bracket, special interests and so on.

- If you want to attract business executives as clients, there is no point in submitting a press release to *Woman & Home* magazine. If you want working mums as clients, then don't approach *Management Today*.

- There are four annual publications you may find useful: *Writers' and Artists' Year Book*, *The Writer's Handbook*, *The Guardian Media Guide* and *The Freelance Photographers' Handbook*. They all contain a wealth of information, names and addresses. Your local bookshop or library will have them.

- Professional PR agencies use *Willings Press Guide* or *PIMS* – but these cost megabucks and are not really necessary. However, you may find it useful to browse through a copy in a library and pick out relevant contacts.

- A local story will sometimes be picked up by the national media – so be prepared. It may never happen to you – but it could!

ACTION PLAN

Write a press release here. Keep it to around 250 words but no more than one page of A4 in double-line spacing. Do it now. Tomorrow, make it your mission to find the names and contact details of all the local newspapers in your area or county. Do the same for local radio and TV stations.

TEN REASONS WHY A PRESS RELEASE IS
THE BEST 'FREE' ADVERTISING OF ALL

1. It really is free.

2. Even if you pay to have it written, you can expect a much larger mention.

3. Editorial is trusted by readers more than advertisements.

4. Editorial is usually read; advertisements are often skipped.

5. Editors have pages to fill, so you are actually helping them.

6. Readers believe that editorial space is earned on merit, while adverts are paid for.

7. In the right publication, your business can have a perceived 'upmarket' image.

8. They are simple and quick to write – but simple doesn't mean easy.

9. They are cheap to distribute by fax or email.

10. The publication pays for typesetting, so you don't have to.

TIP

Make PR part of your weekly routine.

TEN TIPS TO HELP YOU PRESENT YOUR PRESS RELEASE

You can send your press release by post with a covering letter, or call the news desk and ask if you can send a press release by email.

1. Keep to one sheet of A4 if possible. More will reduce your chances of even being considered. Editors will ask for more if they need it.

2. Type or print on one side only. Use double-line spacing.

3. If you are posting, send only pristine, perfect, first-generation copies.

4. Ensure that your name appears on every sheet. (Use the 'header' facility if you have a word processor.)

5. Editors can spot a blatant advert masquerading as a press release from a hundred paces.

6. Keep sentences and paragraphs short.

7. Check, double-check and triple-check spelling.

8. Avoid fancy fonts or typeface – Times New Roman is ideal. Stick to black ink and avoid jokes, cartoons, illustrations, graphs or charts.

9. If you are posting it, include a brief covering letter. Keep it simple and address it to a named person. Do not pester editors by asking if they received it. They will let you know if they plan to use it.

10. If you do send it by email, put your address, phone and other contact details at the top of the release. Do not transmit the release as an attachment. If you have pictures available, do not send them until you are asked to.

TEN THINGS YOUR PRESS RELEASE MUST
(AND MUST NOT) CONTAIN

1. It *must* have a headline. You have about two seconds to attract the editor's attention. If the headline fails to grab, the rest of your press release will not be read.

2. It *must not* be a blatant advertisement for your company or service. If it is construed as such, it will not be published. Instead, you may receive many calls from the advertising departments inviting you to buy advertisements.

3. It *must* have a news angle. For example, this may be to announce a new product or service, to mark the anniversary of something, to mention a famous name visiting your area, to announce new and improved offices, to announce the youngest, oldest, rarest or most unusual of something, to announce a prestigious new client (with that client's permission).

4. It is OK to be inventive when looking for a news angle. News in this instance can mean topical.

5. If your press release is more than one page long, every sheet *must* have an identifier key word or catch line to grab the reader's attention.

6. Include your details, especially how you can be contacted, and number the pages if there are more than one.

7. At the foot of each sheet except the last one put '/more' if the text is continued.

8. At the foot of the last sheet put – 'ENDS' – and the correct word count.

9. It will help your chances of success if you add a standard form of 'notes for editors' after 'ENDS' that explain the background to your company or your industry.

10. You must not use registered trademarks, brand names, individuals' names or quotations without the prior written consent of their owners, even if they are clients.

5. ADVERTISING

Advertising can work, in spite of the naysayers, but you have to get it right.

'Buying a hole in a page and pouring money into it' is how advertising is sometimes described. So often you will hear people say, 'Advertising doesn't work. Forget it, waste of money, doesn't work.' Of course it works! You have only to open any newspaper or magazine, turn on the television, turn on the radio and advertisements are everywhere. Advertising does work and the people who tell you it doesn't are doing it wrong. They are the ones who spend a small fortune and gain very little, if anything, in return. However, if you get it right, advertising can work dramatically to help build your business.

I have sold and bought advertising for many years and here is my guide on how to do it properly, how to get it right, so it will bring in business. Not only will I show you how to avoid mistakes, I will also tell you the secrets of how to save money on advertising as well, which I have learned sometimes through hard experience.

 **Extensive research proves that response increases with the frequency with which an advertisement appears.**

When taking out an advert in a newspaper or magazine, never allow yourself to be talked into buying expensive display advertising at 'rate card' prices. There is no proof that a big advertisement works any better than a small one. Think small and consider using classified columns. Extensive research proves that response increases with the frequency with which an advertisement appears. You may get few calls from your first classified advertisement but, when you repeat it a week later, there will be more interest. This increases over the third and fourth weeks, then tails off. Leave it for a week or two, then repeat the cycle and expect another upsurge of response. If the ad 'bombs' first time around, change it – don't run the same ad again.

Readers may see your advertisement in week one and do nothing. The next week, they see it again, plan to call you but forget. The following week, they do actually call. For some people it may be as long as a month before they remember having seen your advert. They will then actively look for it and get in touch.

One of the most powerful words in advertising is 'free'. Think about what you can offer readers as an inducement to call. You can advertise without spending vast amounts of money by identifying your potential clients and thinking about what might interest them. If this seems difficult, think of them as people like you who share your interests.

The whole point here is to advertise in the places these people are going to see, and consequently, to respond to, your advertisement. For example, some of our coaches have built their entire practice on obtaining permission to display a tasteful and professional notice at a local health club or gymnasium. The members usually have an interest in their own development as well as the disposable income to pursue it. Coaching fits perfectly into their lifestyle and aspirations. Sports clubs and special-interest organisations offer similar opportunities.

If a particular advertisement is not working, do not throw it out. It may be that all you have to do is tweak the headline very, very slightly and you can alter the impact. We did tests in Australia and found that adding one word boosted the response. It was incredible. The phones rang off the hook simply because we added the word 'mate'!

ACTION PLAN

Use this page to write and design your own brief classified advertisement for your business. Get quotations for classified space from each of the local newspapers you listed.

TEN TOP TIPS ON SAVING ADVERTISING MONEY
THAT THE MEDIA DON'T WANT YOU TO KNOW

1. Never pay the 'rate card' price for adverts – always negotiate their 'best' price.

2. Ask for a 'forward features' list and advertise in issues that mention your speciality.

3. Invite sales reps to contact you with low, low prices if an advertiser drops out.

4. If they won't drop the price, ask for a free upgrade to a bigger advert.

5. Don't pay premium extras for 'special positions' – they don't necessarily work any better.

6. Don't pay extra for colour – it rarely looks as good as you expect it to.

7. Seek generous discounts for a series of ads – again, ignore the rate card.

8. Seek deep discounts for 'payment with order'.

9. Provide camera-ready copy and seek a reduction for this.

10. Prices fall as deadlines approach – book as late as you dare.

TIP

One of the best advertising deals I ever got was for a £4,000 magazine ad. They wouldn't negotiate, so I sent my artwork with a cheque for £2,000 attached and a message saying, 'Run the ad if you have a space and cash the cheque ... if you can't fit me in, please return my cheque.' Surprise, surprise, a space magically appeared and the ad was run at this 50 per cent discount. It's hard to say 'no' when they're holding a cheque in their hand!

6. REFERRALS

A happy client will gladly refer someone else to you.

The best thing about referrals is that they cost nothing at all. So how do you get them? You just ask. At what point do you ask? Once you've supplied your product or service, you approach your customer and simply ask politely if they know anyone who might also require the services of your company.

Do not follow up the lead with, 'Would you let them know about me?' The truth is that they never will or, at the very best, they might, if they remember. You need to be in the driving seat. Ask your client if they can give you the names and contact details of six friends, colleagues, relatives or associates who might benefit from using your services. Then ask permission to contact them with a special offer, using your client's name as a means of getting your foot in the door. Be bold and ask for six names – you may get two. If you ask for two, you may get none and your client may feel that they have let you down. You do not want this to happen.

After asking for a referral, take the bull by the horns and ask your happy customer for a testimonial. A testimonial is a third-party endorsement. Whenever a client says something nice to you, ask them if they would mind putting their remarks in writing for you. Most will agree, especially if they have something to gain by having their name passed around positively. It is someone else saying that you are good, rather than you.

 Testimonials from satisfied clients are among the most powerful tools in your marketing portfolio.

Testimonials from satisfied clients are among the most powerful tools in your marketing portfolio. They are very nearly, but not quite, as good as word-of-mouth recommendations, but they do tend to have a longer shelf life. You could say it yourself but it would sound egocentric.

When someone else says great things about you, they will be believed. They have paid money, used your services and worked with you. Using testimonials in your marketing literature is another way of reducing the risk to potential clients. If someone else has tried your service and recommends it, it offers a potential client something tangible to use to judge the quality of your service.

Most customers you approach will never have written a testimonial for anyone before. People tend to shy away from things they haven't done before, so you simply ask, 'Can I jot that down and read it back to you to make sure it's exactly what you said? May I put that on my website? Would you be OK with that and can I put your name against it? Otherwise, people will think I've just made it up.'

Most satisfied customers will agree and be happy for you to use their name but, to prevent any comebacks, you need to take the following steps:

1. The originals must be kept safely in case you ever need to prove their authenticity.

2. They must be signed and dated for the same reason and, to prevent any problems at a later date, you are advised to ask the person giving them to confirm in writing that you have their permission to use them for your promotional purposes.

3. Always respect the confidentiality of your clients and, even if you cannot use their full name, ask if you can limit their identity to initials and county when you use their glowing comments in your advertising or on your website.

It would be nice to have a testimonial from every single client but three or four is ideal. You can go overboard, as I did. At one point, I had more than a thousand testimonials on my company website. I thought it was so impressive! When I realised that people just don't read them all, I reduced them to a dozen of the best. Referrals and testimonials must be freely given. You must never pressure your clients to get them. When you do contact a potential referee, do so with sensitivity, since you are putting your clients' professionalism and reputation on the line, as well as your own.

ACTION PLAN

Instead of throwing out junk mail when it drops through your letter-box, read it and see how the sender uses testimonials. Use the best as your template. From this moment on, ask for testimonials whenever a client or customer says something positive about you.

7. THE INTERNET

**If you have a business you *must* have a website.
It is your shop window to the world.
There are very few exceptions.**

Once you have your website up and running, do not expect the world to beat a path to your door. They won't. It takes time and networking to build up traffic to your site. You need to get a reputation. You need to spread the word using all the marketing tricks I have described so far: networking, public relations, getting on the radio and into print as well as advertising. In fact, anything to get your domain name known.

Five years ago, the Coaching Academy did not have a website. Someone persuaded me I should have one, so I got one but spent the tiniest amount of money possible on having it designed. That was a daft mistake. My website was so awful it let the company down. Prices for building a website have come down so much lately that setting up a professional-looking site is no longer expensive. However, remember that this is a marketing tool that has to work for you. It is not an advert to show off the web builder's skills at putting together a site with more special effects than anyone else's. It is there to generate business by selling direct from the site or to generate enquiries for you.

A website is like direct mail, but from the Internet, and, as with direct mail, you want people to open up the envelope, read the letter from start to finish and do something at the end. You want them either to pick up the phone or make an approach, perhaps by filling in a questionnaire. Your website should have the same effect. It is there to stimulate activity, not to impress with clever graphics. If you follow a simple formula, you can't go wrong.

A lot of people spend months designing their website. It is not necessary. The best website for teaching people how to put together a website is Gary Halbert's site at www.thegaryhalbertletter.com. Gary Halbert is an American direct-mail copywriter and he is brilliant at what he does. His site has the simplest of formats. It appears on your computer screen like a typed letter on a piece of cream paper. You scroll down and you have two options: 'Read Archived Newsletters' and 'Subscribe to Receive Updates on New Newsletters'. It is a fantastic resource, much of it free, not only for putting together your own website but also for how to sell through direct mail.

Having a website means you have the opportunity to make money while you are asleep. It gets you away from trading your time for money. You can be doing other things in the knowledge that money is coming in from another source. I learned this from a coach I know. He was not actually trained at the Coaching Academy (what *was* he thinking?) but I like to put him on a pedestal because he is a great coach who had the dedication to sit down for several weeks and write a six-part course on coaching.

He did not know much about websites, so he hired someone to build one for him. He sells each course for £12.99 or $19.99 in the States. He says, 'It's brilliant. I wake up in the morning and check my inbox to see all the orders that have come in from America through the night.' He has so many hits on his sites that he sells banner adverts to other people involved in coaching, though he makes sure it is to businesses that do not conflict with his enterprise. Advertisers get business from the banners and they come back month after month, year after year. He makes £50,000 a year from his website. Most people would be incredibly happy just to do that, but it also creates clients for his business.

He also gives talks on coaching to groups, which he edits and puts on to 45-minute tapes, and sells them for £9.99.

 We are all in a global market place now and there is no reason why your company should not trade outside the UK and make money for you without having to trade time for cash.

We are all in a global marketplace now, and there is no reason why your company should not trade outside the UK and make money for you without having to trade time for cash.

MAKING YOUR WEBSITE WORK: AN EXAMPLE

A person sets up a business importing Italian furniture into the UK and sells it through her website. To sell her stock worldwide, the owner needs to make sure that, when potential customers go onto the Internet and key in 'Italian furniture' in a search engine, her company comes high up on the sites listed in the results. In order to do this, she needs to hire a web-placement company. It really is worth the money, because there is no point in having a website that no one can find. If you had a shop that nobody ever walked past you would soon go bust.

This is a niche business and no one is going to buy just one piece of Italian furniture. If they like Italian chairs and tables they are going to want to furnish the whole room or even the entire house with the line. You need a very visual website where the whole catalogue can be seen online. However, the difficulty with selling furniture on the Web is that it is hard to see from a photograph just how big the piece is. Even if you print the sizes, it is still difficult to imagine how it would look in your home, so the website could include a virtual planning facility. By putting in the dimensions of a room and, using the mouse on a computer, positioning the furniture, the customer will see just how it would look in their home.

The supplier gives a thirty-day money-back guarantee or even a thirty-day free trial. If a particular piece of furniture doesn't look right in your room, if it's too big, too small or the wrong colour, the supplier will come and pick it up free of charge, as long as the item is not damaged. If it is, you pay for it. The idea should be to get a piece of furniture into the customer's hands as effortlessly as possible. Once they have got that piece in their room and they are living with it, they will want to add to the collection, perhaps by ordering a bookcase or coffee table.

The customer hands over their credit card for 'shipping purposes' and at, say £25, the shipping is still subsidised but it avoids customers who are complete timewasters. When the time comes to charge for the furniture, the supplier already has their credit card details on the computer. At the end of the thirty days, the customer either loves it and pays for it or doesn't and the supplier takes it away. Surely, that's a far better way of selling than saying to the customer, 'You pay your money, you take the risk and it's just tough if you don't like it.'

As part of the process, the customer is also signed up to an electronic newsletter about Italian furniture. In one letter, the owner tells her customers that she has been on a buying trip to Italy and found the most delightful corner cupboard – a small piece of furniture that will turn any dead space into something that friends and family will admire. The newsletter continues,

> We have instructed our importers to supply stock to us in the UK on 1 August and, because they are a new supplier, we are limited to only 50 units. We are taking advance orders now and, if you would like to reserve one, please reply to this email now. We already have your details on our database and, by 5 August, you will have one of these cupboards sitting in your living room. If it is not perfect, tell us and we will come and pick it up. If you like it, we will simply charge your card.

By telling customers that the cupboard is scarce, they are encouraging people to buy now rather than later. Will they sell all fifty units? They will probably sell five hundred! It is entirely ethical. Do you really think that when you go to a 'closing-down sale' there are only seventy rugs left? No, they have seven hundred more in the stockroom. We all know it is a sales gimmick but I would not be willing to take the risk of missing out on the first fifty.

Now the customer has bought two items of furniture, proved they love Italian furniture and, just as important, their creditworthiness, so they qualify for the Italian Furniture Discount Club. Membership entitles them to 10 per cent off the published price and an advance update on new stock coming into the country.

Then the customer receives another newsletter by email telling them that the company has acquired a batch of vases at a very special price and they will receive one free. All they need do is forward the attachment about the company to five friends or colleagues who might be interested in Italian furniture. The email says,

> You may know people who have been to your house and admired your furniture. Perhaps it is someone who has just moved and wants to furnish their new home. Whatever the reason, send the attachment to five people. Email us when you have done so and we will ship the vase to you. You don't have to prove that you have done it, we will take it on trust!

Are people going to take the vase and not forward the email? I don't think so. They are satisfied customers. For the price of a cheap vase and shipping, the company is beginning to build up a wonderful relationship with its customers. If it looks after these people, gives them good value and honours its promises, it is going to have a great business.

Why stop at furniture? The company now has customers who love something classy and are prepared to pay for it. The company can easily expand into fine art, perhaps jewellery, and into the rest of the world.

ACTION PLAN

Look at a whole range of websites. Decide which you think work and which don't. Return to the ones you liked and note the features they included. Use the Internet to do comparative window shopping for prices on domain registration, website hosting and design. If you do not have email, sign up now.

8. WRITE A NEWSLETTER

A regular newsletter can be a powerful means of keeping your business in the public eye.

'What is the point of having a newsletter?' you may ask. A newsletter is a continuous reminder about your business. You can either print it and post it out to your customers or distribute it by email. I used to believe the former was better, but now I would say that email is the better way of doing it. It is faster and cheaper. You can send your newsletter out free or you can charge a subscription – the choice is yours. Your mailing list is made up of everyone who has ever enquired about your services, whether they became clients or not, including everyone whose business card you have collected and everyone to whom you have sent your brochure. Your newsletter is a valuable free bonus. It can be time-consuming to write on a regular basis, so do not be too ambitious by planning an eight-page weekly epic. Some recipients may see a weekly bulletin as irritating, so a monthly publication might be better with a quarterly issue as an alternative; or you could give the customer or potential customer a choice of frequency.

The secret of writing a good newsletter is the same as that for a testimonial or any kind of promotional material: keep it interesting. Write about people you've worked with, new contracts; include testimonials and explain how you can provide the same standard of service for the reader. You can also tell them about cut-price offers, discounts for prompt payment of bills and any public presentations or exhibitions that you have planned. If you've done a presentation and someone has reviewed it, include it in the newsletter with a credit for the source. It is all about building your credibility and building relationships.

When you are out collecting business cards at networking events, ask if you can send them a newsletter. 'I don't want to bombard you with stuff but would you like me to put you on the distribution list. I don't charge for it but you will receive our newsletter. Is that OK with you?' 'Yes, that's absolutely fine,' they will reply. There's another potential customer!

Some prospective clients can take months before they decide to use a particular service. If they receive a monthly or quarterly newsletter about your company with any seasonal offers, you will be ensuring that your contact name and details are sent to them regularly. It makes good marketing sense. When they are ready for your service it will be your company they contact.

Just because the people you met at the Chamber of Commerce meeting on Monday night seemed very interested at the time but there has been no follow-through, it doesn't mean that they won't in the future. Your job is to maintain an ongoing relationship, so, when the timing is right for them, you are uppermost in their minds.

I know coaches who send their newsletters to potential clients by email and at the bottom they ask them to forward it to anyone they think might be interested.

You should also give people the option to opt out of receiving your newsletter.

ACTION PLAN

Think about your newsletter.

How often will you publish? ☐ monthly? ☐ quarterly?

How will you publish? ☐ paper? ☐ email? ☐ both?

Will it be free? If not, what price? ☐ free ☐ cost £_____

List 50 people to send your newsletter to:

1. _____	27. _____
2. _____	28. _____
3. _____	29. _____
4. _____	30. _____
5. _____	31. _____
6. _____	32. _____
7. _____	33. _____
8. _____	34. _____
9. _____	35. _____
10. _____	36. _____
11. _____	37. _____
12. _____	38. _____
13. _____	39. _____
14. _____	40. _____
15. _____	41. _____
16. _____	42. _____
17. _____	43. _____
18. _____	44. _____
19. _____	45. _____
20. _____	46. _____
21. _____	47. _____
22. _____	48. _____
23. _____	49. _____
24. _____	50. _____
25. _____	
26. _____	

TEN WAYS TO CREATE A NEWSLETTER THAT CREATES CLIENTS

1. Create a newsletter that lets prospective clients know what you do and keeps existing clients loyal.

2. Give your newsletter a catchy title or at least one that says something about your business.

3. A newsletter is not just a very long advertisement. Ensure it contains information.

4. Let your newsletter reflect the personality of your practice.

5. Send your newsletter by first-class post – this implies added value and shows that you care.

6. Use A4 paper and ensure good-quality reproduction (laser print or high street quick-copy shops).

7. Include offers that are 'exclusive' to newsletter readers. This encourages them to read them.

8. Look at examples of newsletters that appeal to you and copy their layout.

9. Put a cover price on the front page (at least £1), but send the newsletter free with your compliments. This adds perceived value.

10. Avoid fancy fonts, especially if you send your newsletter by email – what leaves your computer will not always be what is received at the other end. Also, make sure the email attachment is not too large, since it can clog up some mailers and annoy the recipient, especially if they are not on broadband.

9. JOINT VENTURES

Joint ventures are an effective and virtually free way of gaining the most valuable marketing edge of all – word-of-mouth recommendation.

In big business, a joint venture is sometimes called a *strategic alliance*, but a joint venture is simply working with other people towards a common goal. You team up with someone in a noncompeting but related business where you can cross-refer clients. To do this, you write a letter to everyone on their client database as if it were from your joint-venture partner, and they (or you) mail it out to their clients. In return, you allow them access to your own list of prospects and clients through you. It could not be simpler. However, do beware of falling into the trap of creating and distributing junk mail, and observe the data-protection rules.

The key to success in joint ventures is to give as good as you get and to be a partner, not a user. If, between you, you have two hundred customers on your respective databases, that makes two hundred clients who have used either company. Hopefully, you will have done a great job and, when you write to them, they will read the letter with interest because you've already proved your worth.

You could write a joint-venture letter like this:

Dear Phillip

The reason I am writing to you today is to introduce you to my friend and colleague Jonathan Smith. Jonathan is a professional coach. This means he helps individuals within an organisation to identify their goals and achieve them faster than if they were working by themselves.

Research has shown that coaching within an organisation will improve motivation, decrease staff attrition and increase productivity. Over the next couple of weeks, Jonathan has made some space in his diary to take on some new clients. I would strongly recommend that you call him as soon as possible to book a no-obligation consultation for your company.

Please mention my name when you do so, so he can give you the special introductory offer agreed with him for my clients, who, I believe, would benefit from his extremely valuable service.

Yours sincerely

You then send this letter out to names on your business partner's database. You pay the postage and the photocopying because that is only fair. I guarantee the phone will ring far more than if you had just written to those companies yourself. It is because the letter comes from someone they know, trust, have already paid money to and respect. It is an endorsement that will work.

You need to work out between yourselves a method of payment for business that comes from the joint venture. You could either swap goods and services or come to a financial arrangement with a commission for each lead that develops from your joint deal. If you are working together towards a common goal, it's far easier than doing it alone. You do not have to limit yourself to one joint venture, either. The more people you team up with the better. My coaches arrange alliances with local personal trainers, dentists or management consultants and below I have listed some other examples of joint ventures that might work very well.

LANDSCAPE GARDENER AND ESTATE AGENT

When we move into a new home, we like to add our own touch. Likewise, when we have a garden, we like to 'make it our own'. However, typically, it involves manual work and you can get your hands very dirty. A perfect joint venture could involve the estate agent who sells the home and a landscape gardener (or just a straightforward gardener). The estate agent might say, 'I know many of my clients spend time decorating their new homes and it can take a year or so to get around to the garden. Some clients have found that the perfect solution is to hire someone to avoid the delay and stress by quickly turning the garden into a work of art. However, when you move into a new area, it's difficult to know the difference between the cowboys and the honest workers. For the past year, I've been recommending a small, family-run company that's never let anyone down. You call them, they'll come over, give you a quotation without obligation and they won't tread mud into your house, either. If you mention my name when you call, they'll give you ten per cent off.'

A good gardener can easily work from referrals and build a business by creating a relationship like this with half a dozen local estate agents.

Perhaps the agents could be compensated with a '10 per cent of all fees billed' deal, which would provide them with a stream of income even after they've sold the house. This way, the gardener knows that his/her marketing costs will never exceed 10 per cent of income. Of course, the gardener could have a reciprocal arrangement with the agent. If, for example, a client is smartening up their garden in anticipation of selling their property, the gardener could tell them about the estate agent and the special rate that is offered to his clients.

Estate agents can (and do) refer dozens of different services, from carpet fitters to decorators to kitchen designers, and get commission from them all.

GRAPHIC DESIGNER AND A SOLICITOR

A solicitor typically deals with situations involving change, including divorces, house moves (which could well be triggered by a divorce) and selling and buying businesses, which may need the services of a good graphic designer. New business stationery, new corporate images, home letterheads, change-of-address cards – all may be needed when change occurs, and the solicitor is the first person to know when there are people going through change.

A great relationship would be to find solicitors who specialise in mergers and acquisitions and convince them that they are doing their clients a service by introducing them to a top-quality graphic designer who can also look after all their printing. Due to client confidentiality, the solicitor would give their client the designer's details and let them get in contact if they wished.

When someone buys a new home they might be in need of new cards or letterheads. When someone starts a new business these are usually the first things on the shopping list, so a graphic designer could get dozens of referrals from solicitors, but what would the solicitors get in return? Perhaps a completely free overhaul of their own corporate identity – which most solicitors sorely need!

A HEALTH-FOOD BUSINESS AND A GYM

The synergy here is obvious. Customers of a health-food business are clearly interested in improving their health, and improving their fitness is just one step away. The clients of a gym will be encouraged to eat in a healthy way by their personal trainers and a joint venture between these two businesses is a natural and obvious marriage. However, far too many businesses try to do everything by themselves instead of sharing the load.

ACTION PLAN

▨ List at least twenty organisations that you could approach as a joint venture.

▨ Draft a letter that you could invite them to send out to their clients so that the intentions are clear.

▨ Remember to answer the reader's question, 'What's in it for me?'

▨ Also, think about what you will offer your joint-venture partners in return.

10. PUBLIC SPEAKING

This marketing method is not only free but you may even be paid for your efforts.

Nearly every town has several membership organisations to which a speaker will be invited to give a presentation at one of their monthly meetings. Some are charitable organisations and others have a business or specific professional base. They provide you with a captive audience, so captivate them with your Sack Your Boss Revolution story. Tell them how you became disenchanted with working for someone and the amazing story of how you set up your business. If you are not used to talking to an audience, I suggest you make a short presentation, then hold a question-and-answer session.

You know all about sacking your boss by now because you have read most of the book, and you know more about your company than anyone else. You are well prepared, so you will be able to tackle any question. Make a virtue of your weakness by telling your audience that you always think interactive sessions are far more interesting than having someone just lecture them.

At the end of your talk put into practice your new networking skills. Don't just tell your audience, 'You know how to get hold of me. If you want me, give me a call.' Avoid this 'fingers crossed' approach and invite your audience to leave their business cards so you can send them a copy of your free newsletter.

If you are in a business where you take on clients, such as a financial consultancy, accountancy, law or coaching, do not trust it to luck to obtain new business from a speaking engagement. You could try this method of consolidating your contacts.

Take a large pad and divide the page into time slots.

> Nine o'clock
> Ten o'clock
> Eleven o'clock
> Noon

… and so on.

At the end of your discussion hold up the pad and say something like, 'We've been talking now for about forty-five minutes and I can tell from your reaction and your questions that this a subject that interests many of you. The problem is that I have very little time to take on new clients as I have a very packed diary, but what I do once a month is set aside a single day to meet prospective new clients, people who are genuinely interested in hiring me. Please note the "genuinely interested" is because I set aside only one day. I will happily talk to you about other things at any other time, but I set only that one day aside to talk to people who are interested in retaining me.'

Wave your pad and add, 'I have a pad here with time slots for that day, and if you would like to discuss the possibility of my working for you, please fill your name and your best contact number beside your chosen time slot. I'll call you on that day and we can discuss your needs. There are only eight slots available. Where would you like me to start passing that round the room?'

Where the hands go up fastest, the pad goes over there and it whizzes round the room. As the pad comes back you will have eight or nine people who have publicly committed, saying, 'Yes, I am seriously interested in hiring you.' Since you have already mentioned your fees, there are no surprises and no way they can wriggle out later by claiming you are too expensive. If the question of your fee structure does not come up, simply introduce it yourself.

 You have only a certain amount of time every day and every week, so focus on people who are going to become clients rather than use a scattergun approach.

What if you pass your clipboard round and you get only two or three names? It does not matter because it is better than the forty people in the room phoning you the next day and saying. 'Oh, I've got a question about …' You have only a certain amount of time every day and every week, so focus on people who are going to become clients rather than use a scattergun approach.

If you run a business such as a beauty salon or are an osteopath, you might want to offer a complimentary session but a lot of people tell me they don't get many clients from free treatments or sessions. That's because they do complimentary sessions for the wrong people. Do them for those who are interested in hiring you, not for timewasters or the types who will do anything to get something for nothing. You want seriously interested people. Otherwise, you will be wasting your time. You will become frustrated and end up demotivated.

When you interview the people on your list, remember they are finding out whether they want to hire you, but you are also looking at whether you want them as clients. You don't have to take them on. It is your choice. Ultimately, who you do business with is up to you. The polite way to get rid of potential clients you feel might be a problem is to suggest, 'I take on only clients that I feel I can achieve great success with and I'm not sure whether we are going to be matched on this occasion.'

Public speaking and networking will dramatically increase your chances of success. The more you do it, the easier it becomes and the better you get at it, but be prepared for the odd disappointment. Sometimes, you can turn up for a presentation and there will be only a small group, but you should do it anyway. I always tell my students, 'Never vanish as soon as you've finished your talk, but make time to speak to every person who wants to speak to you.'

I once turned up as a guest speaker and there was just one person in the room, but I still gave my talk. Halfway through, I had a bit of a dilemma because my 'audience' got up and went to the toilet. Normally, if this happens, you carry on with your speech. So did I carry on? Did I wait for him to come back? No, I went with him to the Gents' and then carried on when we returned.

ACTION PLAN

▧ Take a sheet of paper and expand your twenty-second elevator speech into a thirty-minute presentation.

▧ Start with an introduction followed by five more segments of five minutes each.

▧ List key words, subjects or topics for each section, then write a short conclusion that leaves your audience on a high.

▧ Research and list ten organisations you could approach to offer your services to as a speaker.

11. TRADE SHOWS

Trade shows are a great way to make your name known to potential customers.

If you go down the trade-show route, do not take a stand in the early days. Visit other people's stands instead. If you do a trade show at a major exhibition hall, hire a booth about the size of a telephone box. Venues like London Olympia and the National Exhibition Centre can be prohibitively expensive unless you are able to share the costs with another business. Of course, you do not have to book stand space. Why not offer your services to the organisers as a workshop speaker in one of their seminar theatres? If you do book a stand, opt for 'space-only' deals and beware of hidden extras such as compulsory public-liability insurance, the use of power points, furniture and fascia boards.

TEN WAYS TO GAIN MOST FROM TRADE SHOWS AND EXHIBITIONS

1. Never pay the rate-card price for a stand – negotiate terms.

2. Never hire extras other than a single electrical power point.

3. Book 'space-only' schemes rather than 'shell schemes' (ready-made stands).

4. Seek a ground-floor spot in a high-traffic area near an entrance, cafés or toilets.

5. Have something moving on your stand to attract attention.

6. Get off your stand and herd the visitors towards it – bribe them with a sweet or a competition.

7. Have a second person on the stand to deal with those you present to them.

8. Use your most dynamic and attractive 'personality-plus' staff.

9. Offer a discount: 'If you book at this show …'

10. Make it obvious what you do.

TEN WAYS TO TURN YOUR ATTENDANCE AS AN EXHIBITION VISITOR TO YOUR ADVANTAGE

1. Always visit on two consecutive days.

2. Always wear a distinctive colour on both days – red is good.

3. Get there early on the first day and visit as many stands as you can.

4. Talk to as many stand staff as you can – buy nothing and refuse leaflets.

5. Visit early again on the second day – you will be recognised and greeted as a 'friend'.

6. Lie low over the lunch period but talk to as many people as you can in the café.

7. Give out your business cards as freely as possible – to other visitors and stand staff.

8. Your objective is to find potential clients or strategic alliances.

9. Sympathise with tired stand staff – they will then see you as 'one of them'.

10. Visit special stands just before closing time to say a personal 'goodbye'.

TIP

Always follow up all enquiries the next day.

12. LEAFLETS AND BROCHURES

Leaflets and brochures are a great way to get the benefits of your business before the eyes of potential clients or customers.

You *must* have something to give people at trade fairs or when you are at a public-speaking engagement. A simple leaflet printed on one side of an A5 sheet can be cheap to create and reproduce. It can be mailed out, pinned on club or work notice boards (always seek permission first) and given to anyone who asks, so always carry them in your pocket, handbag or car. You never know when a great opportunity will arise.

One step up from a leaflet is your brochure. This can be a single sheet of A4 size, it can be folded or you can really let your imagination run wild and create an entire information pack. You will need to spell out the benefits of your business, your specialist areas and how the business works. You must clearly include your contact details and you will gain a greater response if you give a few background notes about who you are and where you are coming from.

TIP

Place your promotional literature in the exhibitors' press room – organisers rarely (if ever) check these.

ACTION PLAN

■ Over the next few days, collect as many leaflets and brochures as you can from competitors in your line of business.

■ See which ones work for you and which do not.

■ Close your eyes for a few minutes and visualise the size, shape, colour and feel of your own brochure.

■ Shop around for printing quotes. Prices vary alarmingly and the most costly is not necessarily the best.

■ Think 'black ink' to keep costs down.

■ If you are thinking about adding some colour, speak to your printer about using coloured paper.

■ Listen and ask.

TEN SECRETS OF BROCHURE DESIGN

1. Print your brochure on A4 paper.

2. A double-sided three-fold brochure says 'cheap'. Leave this format for menus in takeaway restaurants.

3. A double-sided brochure folded in half (to give a finished size of A5) looks bigger and classier and fits a standard C5 envelope without further folds.

4. Add quality by using thick paper – at least 100 gsm.

5. Add colour by using black print on tinted paper. You then don't have to pay for coloured inks.

6. Use one consistent font throughout. Vary its size for contrast and create headlines.

7. You must say who you are, where you are, what you do and what it costs.

8. You must tell readers what to do next and make it easy for them to do it.

9. Use a single column on the front and back pages – clean and simple to attract interest.

10. Use double or triple columns on inside pages, because it makes your brochure look more informative.

TIP

People buy from people. Consider using a good-quality head-and-shoulders photograph of yourself but don't let your brochure become an ego trip.

TIP

You can double the response rate when you include a reply postcard or coupon that a potential customer can complete for more information.

13. WRITE A 'REPORT'

A report makes you stand out from the crowd, making you look like an expert in your field.

At some point, you should write a 'Special Report'. It can be as long or as short as you want, perhaps between one and two thousand words, on an aspect of your business or your industry. It will take you a couple of evenings to do but you will enjoy doing it. Your report does not need glossy covers, full colour or fancy graphics. A few pages of good, practical information, photocopied and stapled in one corner, will do the trick. Get someone to read it through and make sure it looks professional, is written in good English and is correctly punctuated.

You are probably asking, 'Why, when I'm already devoting every hour I can to the business, should I spend a few evenings writing a report? I'm not a teacher.' It is true, you are not a teacher but, by writing a report, you will stand out from the crowd. You will be regarded as an expert in your field. Only experts write reports and experts tend to be paid more than people who aren't experts.

People love something for nothing, so imagine the pulling power when you feature in your advertisement and promotional material, 'For your *free* report – please telephone now.'

How do I get it published? You go to the biggest 'publishers' in the world, a quality print shop in your town or city, and they will photocopy it. That, ladies and gentlemen, is publishing. It simply means getting it into print. Once you have published a report it does a lot for you. It gives you credibility and you can use your report to get extra business for your company. People love something for nothing, so imagine the pulling power when you announce in your advertisement and promotional material, 'For your *free* report – please telephone now.'

When potential customers phone, you will have the chance to find out more about them and they about you. Always follow up within a week of sending out the report. If they have asked for it, they will certainly read it, so be sure to spell out what they must do next: for example, 'Call today to book your free trial session.'

You should put your report on the website and you will start being interactive with your potential clients. When you do your presentations, give out your free reports at the end and make sure you go to your networking events with a pile of reports under your arm. It gives you free publicity. You can also phone your local newspaper and say, 'I've just had a report published and have fifty copies to give away to your readers.' Local press love giving away stuff by local authors, which is what you have suddenly become once you've written a report. Ask if you can save the newspaper time and money by sending out the reports to the competition winners yourself. That way you are back in control of generating enquiries and prospects. Some newspapers will not allow you to have the names and addresses but it is still worth doing because, if people have entered a competition, they are interested in the prize.

Many of my coaches have written reports on coaching with great titles that have caught the imagination of newspapers. Confidence-coaching reports have had titles such as 'The New You, Ooze Confidence' and 'Unleash Your Inner Tiger'. Relationship coaches have written 'Become the Man from Mars' or, alternatively, 'Become the

Woman from Venus'. Even a financial adviser or accountant could write a report that doesn't have to be dull. How about, 'Seven Things You Must Know Before You Invest' or a report entitled 'How to Avoid Losing Your Shirt on Investments'? This one would have mass appeal in a local paper: 'Become a Financial Wizard in Just Thirty Minutes – We Show You How'.

The owner of an evening-wear shop could come up with 'Top Tips on Being the Best-Dressed Person at the Ball', but you would get far more publicity with a free report entitled 'Stand Out from the Crowd with the Secrets that Hollywood Stars Keep to Themselves'.

ACTION PLAN

Take five minutes to think up titles for three free special reports that you could write on your business:

1 _____

_____

_____

_____

2 _____

_____

_____

_____

3 _____

_____

_____

_____

14. WRITING A BOOK

The next step after writing a report is to write your own book. It is not as daunting as it sounds.

If you can talk, you can write. A 200-page book at a page a day will take well under a year to write. There is even a distance-learning course on 'How to Write a Book on Anything in 14 Days or Less'.

Again, an author gains immediate credibility as an expert in their field. You will have as much fame as you can handle but, more important, you will have an incredible marketing tool. Take copies along to any presentation you give. It is a fact that audience members always want more than a speaker can give, so they will be eager to buy copies of your book. You can also offer copies to magazine editors and radio stations as competition prizes.

One coach who did this in a national newspaper had more than a thousand replies. Enough of these were converted into paying clients to fill every slot in the coach's appointment book and there were still some left to refer to other coaches. As a published author, you can command higher fees, too.

ACTION PLAN

Decide when you are going to write your book.

Write the start date here: _____

Write the completion date here: _____

FIVE REASONS WHY YOU SHOULD WRITE A BOOK, EVEN IF YOU ARE NOT A NATURAL AUTHOR

1. Authors are respected. When you write a book about an aspect of your professional life, you will establish instant credibility that can be translated into client fees.

2. You can reach a huge market if you tailor your manuscript accordingly.

3. You have the benefit of hindsight. What do you wish you had known at the time you were starting your business?

4. While your book shouldn't be seen as an income generator, it will certainly be an interest generator, even if it does cost you money (which you can budget into your marketing plans).

5. Your book can also increase your level of customer service. You can send a signed copy to a client with your compliments to thank them for their patronage.

FIVE TIPS FOR WRITING A BOOK

1. The biggest market is for people who have an interest in, but little knowledge of, your profession.

2. You might get lucky and interest a mainstream publisher but, in all probability, you will do better to self-publish. At all costs, avoid 'vanity publishers', who charge you for publishing your own book.

3. Your book should be paperback and about a hundred pages long. Think of about ten possible chapter headings.

4. There are many people who will write your book for you for a fee. It will have your name as author and you alone will know the secret. They are known as 'ghostwriters' because they exist but are rarely seen.

5. If you know a famous person, invite them to write the preface or give you a quote for the cover. Their name alone will add credibility to your book.

15. PROMOTIONS AND PROMOTIONAL MATERIAL

Promotions are a great way to boost business, but so many people let themselves down with their promotional material.

You do not need to spend a huge amount of money on glossy brochures when it comes to promotion. A brilliantly written sales letter on your company paper is just as good as any brochure. Here is a letter I wrote for an imaginary male grooming salon. First, I would buy a mailing list with all the addresses within a mile and a half of the premises and then I would send the following postcard to as many homes in the area as I could afford:

Dear [name of town or suburb] resident

I am writing to you today because you haven't yet visited my new salon and I would like you to. But why should you come here when you probably already have your hair cut elsewhere? May I give you three good reasons?

First, we are proud to offer the highest level of expertise, which means you will come out looking fantastic.

Second, we have all been to hairdressers and barbers where they rush you in and rush you out like cattle. We don't want you to feel like that. In fact, during your session, we are pleased to offer you complimentary refreshments and Danish pastries.

Third, on your first visit we would like to cut your hair at half our published prices. That means you can try us out for just a few pounds.

We do like to book appointments simply because we want to give you the time that you deserve. Please call our freephone number within the next twenty-four hours and book your appointment either for this week or next. Even if it's just for a trim, try us out once, because we want to impress you so much that you will become one of our valued regular clients.

Yours sincerely,

Jonathan

PS Come in this week and we will have champagne on ice waiting for you.

It is simple, but so many new businesses never do promotions to get their venture off the ground with a bang. They just open their door and put a poster in the window. An introductory letter or a postcard would generate instant business and, if the staff do a great job, the salon will have repeat business. As customers claim their first half-price haircut, you can put their name, address and date of birth on your database so the salon can mail them special offers on a regular basis.

About a week before a customer's birthday, the computer could automatically generate a birthday card, signed by the salon owner, which might say, 'Your birthday is just a few days away, so why not come in for that special birthday haircut just so you can look the age you want to be? And, as our birthday present to you, why not treat yourself to a half-price massage while you are here?'

Sending out hundreds of those a week is easy but virtually no one does it. How much does it cost for a few cards, envelopes and stamps. It is much cheaper than taking out an advertisement in the local paper and far more effective. Unless you go totally bald, you will need a haircut every four or five weeks for the rest of your life – but no hairdresser has ever done anything to capture *my* regular business. Many salons just hope people will walk in off the street.

Another easy way of boosting trade for the salon is, as we saw earlier, to approach other businesses in the area. Perhaps you could talk to the local café manager and offer his customers a 25 per cent discount on haircuts. In return, you could give all his staff free haircuts. I have lost count of the number of times I have been to a hotel where you must fill out all your details to check in. So few hotels seem to use that information to send details of special offers, such as 'Why don't you come and spend Valentine's night here and enjoy a free bottle of champagne?' or 'Enjoy a complimentary dinner when you book one of our king-size rooms'. Whatever trade or profession you are in, by being just a bit proactive and using a little ingenuity you can improve your business.

On page 153, I will tell you how only a little growth in three key areas can explode your turnover and dramatically boost your profit.

16. NICHE MARKETING

It is much easier to make money in a niche business, particularly if you are using the Web as one of your major marketing tools.

The last of the Sixteen Pillars of Marketing is niche marketing. If you can identify a specialist area rather than starting up a general business, it will help you stand out from the crowd.

Look at any local sweet shop on your high street. They tend to be small independent companies that sell every type of sweet. Now look at Thornton's. They specialise in chocolates and toffees and they are on virtually every high street in the United Kingdom. When you are next out shopping, why not compare a department store with Moss Bros, who, rather than sell all types of clothing, operate in the niche of evening and wedding hire.

Perhaps you could look at a general sports shop and compare it with, say, Foot Locker, who specialise in sports footwear, or stores that sell only football shirts. Rather than sell every type of sports equipment, they have taken one unique selling point and specialised, since they have found it easier to make money in that area.

Very few people, unless they are on a site such as eBay, make impulse purchases on the Internet, and the Web is fantastic for finding a solution to a problem. If, for example, you are looking for fishing equipment, you will find it at a specialist fishing store, rather than a general sports store where the rods are sold along with bikes, soccer boots and cricket stumps, and it is so easy to find it on the Internet.

I encourage my coaches to become specialists because I am convinced they will make much more money and be far more successful in a niche area such as financial coaching, confidence coaching, corporate coaching, presentation coaching or even relationship coaching. When you are in a niche market, it is a lot easier to target potential customers and, once you have targeted your market and you know where you are aiming, it's a lot easier to hit that target.

Look for your niche in life – but you have to be interested in your chosen area or it will not work.

ACTION PLAN

Use this space to define niche areas you can take your business into. Then list your potential customers.

Niche areas

Potential customers

CHAPTER 9

A CRASH COURSE IN SELLING

There are dozens of excellent books on selling and you should read some of them but, in the meantime, I will give you just a couple of pointers.

If you have people interested in your product or services the next step is to make the sale, but people get scared of selling. They become tense because they feel as though they are almost acting. You do not have to play a part to sell, just be yourself. If you have got this far with your own business, you will already be far more successful at sales than you give yourself credit for.

Whether it was selling the concept of your business to the bank manager or the idea to your partner, you have sold them something – you. If you can get people as excited about your venture as you are, it's great and when you get excited and enthusiastic about things it is actually contagious. The real secret of sales is hard work. The more effort you put in, the more you get out.

Many salespeople believe that thinking about customers or sending an email or two can make sales. The truth is, *you will make a sale only when you are talking to someone*. You cannot do it by telepathy. The salesperson who produces twice as much is the one who works twice as hard, the one who is on that phone talking to customers, rather than shuffling bits of paper, filing, planning what they're doing after work, taking an extended lunch and thinking no one will notice.

You know what? In an office, everyone knows who works the hardest. If you took an anonymous vote in an office on who works the hardest and who works the least and placed everyone else in between, it would be pretty unanimous. The only person who would get it wrong would be the one who works the least. They always think they work the hardest. The salesperson who says, 'I didn't make many sales today' probably didn't make many calls, either. If you make five hundred phone calls a week, even if for half of them you have to leave answer-phone messages, some of them have got to return as sales.

There is a direct link between sales and activity. So, if you're going to start your business with a whimper, don't bother, because it will never happen. Start with a bang! Be active. Talk to people all the time. Go to meetings with people – you never know what may happen. That particular person might not be able to help you but you might be able to ask them who else could. Ask for introductions.

On the whole, people don't mind your using their name. If they find you pleasant, they are not going to mind introducing you to other people. If you're offensive, they're obviously not going to introduce you to anyone, because they won't want to be held responsible for introducing their contacts to a pain in the neck.

WHEN THE PHONE RINGS

So what happens when the phone rings the first time? You panic, unless of course you prepare for what is going to happen. You desperately want to make a sale from that first call. You do not want to blow it, so at least visualise how you will make that sale. Even better, practise with a friend – but first, if you are working from home, have somewhere where you can actually have a professional conversation without hearing kids crying, the washing machine on high spin or someone mowing the lawn outside.

Decide in advance what you are going to say when you pick up the phone, otherwise you will stutter and stammer because you don't have a greeting planned. I would suggest you say something like, 'Good morning. John Smith Organisation. John Smith speaking. How can I help you?' Find out whom you are talking to. You need to take control, so ask, 'Before I go any further, may I just take your name? Great! How do you spell that? Fine. And just in case we get cut off what's a good number to call you back on? Fantastic. Thank you.'

A lot of people, especially in the early days, can get to the end of an entire conversation and have no idea whom they have been talking to. They have been chatting for twenty minutes but haven't struck a deal. Maybe you are too expensive at the moment or perhaps the caller wants time to think it over. You put the phone down without any idea whom you have been talking to because you forgot to ask the person's name. What a waste!

Make sure you ask the caller how they got your number. You need to know where your enquiries are coming from. Was it the presentation that you did? Was it the advertisement in the local paper? Perhaps it was a bit of publicity you generated with your press release. You have to know which of the marketing pillars is working for you.

This is your moment to make an impact. Usually, when someone phones your business, that is the moment when they are in a peak state of interest. That is the moment when they have reached a point at which they are motivated to do something. They may have known about you for a while, they may have seen your advertisement or your publicity, but something made them react today. It is a little bit like walking out of your front door every morning and the gutter drips on your head. It is an irritation or even an annoyance. Then one morning you walk out just as the gutter breaks and you are deluged with water. That is the moment you walk back indoors grab the Yellow Pages and phone the gutter people.

You need to know what it was that triggered their need to find your company or seek out your service. You won't know if you do not ask. It may be something new you have tried in your marketing plan and you have now just hit on the trigger that is going to work for you.

One common mistake business owners make is when they and not their customers decide when the company will be busy. They might say, 'Well, we're always going to be quiet in January and February.' Why? If the rest of the companies in your market decide that January and February are going to be quiet then that's the best time to get business because your competitors aren't even trying. When everyone else is not even bothering to advertise or promote their business, that's the time for you to go for it. There is nothing wrong with bucking the trend. Let me show you how it worked for me.

I do not know any conference company that organises conferences in July and August, since it is traditionally when business is flat because everyone is on holiday. That's a myth because not everyone is on holiday. So I did a promotion in July and August while all my competitors were away. I offered two places for the price of one during the school holidays. I was packed out with people who shared the cost of coming on my courses with a friend.

Everyone loves a discount – give 10 per cent off or even 20 per cent if you can afford it. Perhaps do a buy-one-get-one-free offer.

When you have a new product it is important to stimulate interest. To get people talking about it, you need to start with a bang. It is far better to have a hundred people out there talking about your product than to have just a handful of supporters. The price really is right when you are running a promotion. Everyone loves a discount – give 10 per cent off or even 20 per cent if you can afford it. Perhaps do a buy-one-get-one-free offer, as I did with my summer promotions. But, before you go mad and give it all away, you must have a plan. Sit down and work out the real cost before you go ahead. If you run a buy-one-get-one-free promotion in January, you might get rid of a lot of stock, but your discount is so big that you don't make a profit, which could leave you with a huge cash-flow problem when the bills come pouring in during February and March.

If, once you have done your sums, you realise you cannot afford to discount, don't despair. One of the best things to give away as a special offer is something that appears to have value but costs you nothing. How about giving away advice? All it will cost you is time. A company selling electrical garden tools wanted to boost hedge-trimmer sales so they offered a 'free' personal tutorial on 'getting the best out of your hedge trimmer'. The tutorial included advice on how to look after the machine and tricks of the hedge-cutting trade. The tutorial had a high perceived value, since one-to-one tuition would normally cost £120.

The customer did not have to have their lesson immediately. They could have it at any time in the future. The fact is that hardly anyone ever got round to going for their tutorial, but hedge trimmer sales went up and the promotion cost the company virtually zero.

Recently, I went for my haircut at a salon that had been recommended to me. When I got there I spent quite a bit more than I normally would – in fact an extra 30 per cent – but I didn't mind one bit. It had been referred to me so, before I'd even stepped through the door, I knew I was going to get value for money. They gave me an appointment straightaway, the service was great and I was very pleased with my haircut. As I was leaving they presented me with a small pack of gift cards that I could give to my friends. These cards entitled the recipient to £5 off one male haircut and one female hair appointment. That is a wonderful example of how to bring in new customers at zero cost. That marketing exercise cost next to nothing. When you are charging £50 to £60 for a haircut, a fiver is not going to make a big dent in the income.

ACTION PLAN

Think of ways you could add value to your sales – without giving away your own hard-earned money.

CUSTOMER SERVICE

I must stress that my business is not perfect by any means. All businesses are run by people, and human beings aren't perfect – but, as long as they are striving to do the best they can, they will succeed.

Take the example of the waiter who brings you the wrong order or drops something. If you believe he is genuinely sorry and he's trying his best, you forgive him. Hopefully, your business won't get too many orders wrong or drop too many clangers but, if things do go wrong, what do you do?

The customer is always right? Wrong. The customer is *not* always right, but there is nothing wrong with letting customers *think* they are right. Without customers you don't have a business, so, if you let your customers go away thinking they are right, even when they aren't, then they will have a sense of satisfaction. If you go to great lengths to prove the customer wrong, you will seriously harm your business. Sometimes, you hear people moaning, 'If it weren't for the customers I'd have a fantastic business.' Well, if you have problem customers, maybe you are doing something fundamentally wrong.

TEN WAYS TO DEAL WITH DISSATISFIED CUSTOMERS

1. Listen more than you speak.

2. Empathise (even if they are wrong).

3. Make apologies rather than excuses.

4. Ask what they would like you to do to improve the situation.

5. If appropriate, offer a refund, free further session or another product.

6. If appropriate, offer refunds as vouchers against further services rather than cash.

7. Remember, a dissatisfied client will tell many others. You must be in 'damage-limitation' mode.

8. Never argue, talk over or shout down your client.

9. Let them blow off a head of steam before trying to make your points.

10. Speak slowly, calmly and quietly and maintain your professional demeanour at all times.

Remember, you do not *have* to take someone on as a client or a customer. Many businesses eventually discover that just 20 per cent of their customers, that is two out of every ten, actually bring in 80 per cent of their income. They come to realise that the other 80 per cent of their customers account for only one-fifth of the company's income. So, if you fired 80 per cent of your customers because they create hassle for you, never pay their bills or are always moaning unjustifiably, then you can concentrate on the top 20 per cent and nurture them. So, often when companies re-evaluate their strategy, they discover that they are focusing on the wrong customers. If they focused on the right section of their customer base their business would grow.

THE IMPORTANCE OF CUSTOMER-RELATIONSHIP MANAGEMENT

Customer-relationship management (CRM) means establishing a relationship with your client that goes beyond responding to a simple request for your professional services or to buy your goods. What else can good CRM do for your business and your relationship with your client?

- CRM means getting on first-name terms with your client as soon as it is polite to do so and when both you and your client are comfortable with this.

- CRM means knowing more about your client than you strictly need in order to deliver your service.

- CRM means making your client feel important, listening to their views and opinions, learning what makes them tick.

- CRM means that a client can develop into an acquaintance or even a friend.

A client who is an acquaintance or friend will want you to succeed and will want to help you. What else will this client mean for you and your business?

■ This client will recommend your services as a friend, to a friend.

■ This client will return for related products or additional services.

■ This client will pay promptly.

■ This client will rarely complain. If you do give cause for complaint, deal with the complaint fairly and calmly. A client who receives this treatment can be expected to be even more loyal than one who has never complained.

■ Although exact figures vary, it is generally reckoned that it can cost up to twenty times more to create a new client than retain an existing one. CRM helps you to retain your clients.

■ CRM means treating your clients as you would expect to be treated when you are someone else's client.

The same applies to staff. If you have ten staff you might find two of them outperform the other eight. However, instead of focusing on the top performers, you find that all you are doing is concentrating on the poorest performers who drain your energy, give you a headache and make you wonder why you are in business in the first place. If that is the case, take a long, hard look at your staff. Perhaps it would be better to scale down the business and run it more profitably with just two employees who work brilliantly, who will earn you good money and keep you sane.

CHAPTER 10

GROWING YOUR BUSINESS

Many entrepreneurs find their first customers fairly easily, then, suddenly, the business stops growing.

When someone lent me an audiotape by the American marketing guru Jay Abraham, I first learned the secret of growing a business. There are only three ways to grow your business:

1. increase the number of customers;

2. increase the average size of each sale you make to each customer; and

3. increase the number of times customers come back and buy again.

To do this you:

■ **Increase your customer base** – obviously, attract more customers and you get more business.

■ **Increase the transaction amount for each customer** – get each customer to spend more. That's obvious, too.

■ **Increase the order frequency** to get your customers to buy from you more often, which is also obvious.

However, what is *not* obvious is this. You have to increase each of these things by only a small amount to explode your business income. Now have a look at this simple calculation. Say you have 1,000 customers who buy twice a year from you at £100 a time. By multiplying the number of customers, their spend multiplied by the frequency gives you a total projected income with this formula: $1{,}000 \times £100 \times 2 = £200{,}000$. But, using the same formula, watch what happens if you increase each of these numbers by just 10%: $1{,}100 \times £110 \times 2.2 = £266{,}200$.

An increase of just 10 per cent in all three areas of your business will boost your company's income by *one-third* – 33.1 per cent to be exact. If you were to increase your number of customers, the amount they spend and the frequency with which they buy from you by a quarter, your income would almost *double*. So, by adding 25 per cent, you increase your income from £200,000 to an astonishing £390,625.

Years ago, I worked out this formula when I was doing my stage show. Instead of charging £500 I'd charge £500 plus 10 per cent, and, instead of going to a venue twice a year, which would be typical, I'd somehow try to get myself booked one more time, making it three times a year. I also took on a handful of new venues. Soon I was earning £50,000 a year as a stage hypnotist in my early twenties. The results were amazing, but I was not really doing anything different other than increasing my revenue.

KEEP YOUR HANDS ON THE CASH

As your business grows, you find a lot of people spending your money for you.

Don't ever let other people spend your money. You prevent it by making sure you are the only signatory on the cheques.

Introduce a system whereby a purchase order has to be countersigned before anything is bought, otherwise your staff will be spending your money left right and centre and, before you know it, huge boxes will suddenly start arriving from the stationer's. You will be presented with bills you know nothing about, so you must ensure that, whenever any member of staff purchases items or commissions work such as printing, they always get two quotes. That way you will know whether an item is expensive or not. Put another way, you won't know whether you could have obtained it for half as much elsewhere. I now sign off every purchase order, having learned from experience.

Every time you see something that looks expensive, get a couple more quotes. That way, you will find the staff tend to come back and say, 'Actually, we got it cheaper elsewhere.' Even if you save 10 per cent on everything, that is 10 per cent back in on the bottom line at the end of the year. You've got to be picky about the money, because, if you don't, costs will just run away with you. Everything costs more than you think it will and you never make as much money as you anticipate.

TIP

When you are just starting your business there is a lot to be said for outsourcing as much as you can. Do not buy a photo-copier. Instead, get a company to come and pick up your photocopying and do it for you every week (or every day if you are copying in volume) or drop it around to your local copy shop. As the business grows you must monitor those outsourcing bills. When I discovered my company was spending £900 a month on copying we bought our own photocopier. It paid for itself in six months. Outsourcing is good with small quantities, but when you reach critical mass, bring it back in house.

MANAGING PEOPLE

As your business grows you will have to take on staff, and managing people is the biggest nightmare for any small business owner. Not many people get it right. I have got it wrong so many times that I thought that I had made all the mistakes I could by now. Then I discovered that there are even more mistakes to be made!

Without good people you will not have a good business. In the early days it is tough, because you don't have enough money to hire top staff and you have to 'sell' your business to a potential employee – make them want to join it irrespective of the offered salary – because you aren't in a position to tempt them with money.

Employing your first member of staff is an enormous step. It is all too tempting to employ someone you know because it makes you feel secure. It is probably one of the worst things you can do. People you know well feel they are your equal, rather than an employee. Your authority as the boss will be undermined. They may also take advantage on timekeeping. They will always complain that you are earning more than they are, even though the laws of business say you *have* to earn more than they do so you can pay their wages.

Employing your first stranger is a tough decision. The best person to employ is someone who can do a job you cannot, or is much better at it. Most entrepreneurs are brilliant at selling their product, so you need someone who can do your administration, a person who can sit there, answer the phone efficiently and tidy up after you. Someone who can take care of the dreaded paperwork and keep your accounts up to date.

When I interview someone and they ask about sick pay, it starts to worry me. It may not be the correct human-resources approach but I always ask, 'Do you intend being ill?' They usually reply, 'No, no, no.' 'That's OK,' I say. 'Then you don't have to worry about it.' People who talk about sick pay usually take 'sickies'. If you are a small company you simply cannot afford passengers. I once interviewed someone who was obsessed with sick pay, so I told her that we didn't pay sick leave on a Monday, in order to deter people from not coming in when the weather was good or after they had had a heavy weekend.

Then she replied, 'Oh, no, it wouldn't apply to me. So what happens if I break my leg?'

'Have you ever broken a bone?' I asked.

'No, never,' came the reply.

'Do you ski or do anything like that?'

'No.'

She kept making up all these terrible scenarios and I thought to myself, 'Well if you were self-employed you'd have to work regardless.' Needless to say, she did not get the job because of her attitude.

However, when hiring and firing, it's always important to check the employment rules. The wrong move could cost you a great deal.

Key performance indicators, or KPIs, are the key to successful hiring. I wish I had discovered KPIs a long time ago. Now, whenever I hire someone, I give him or her a letter setting out the KPIs for their job. KPIs set the standard of conduct I expect from my staff. It can either be included in the contract you both sign when you take on an employee, or it can be outlined in a letter of understanding, setting out exactly what is expected.

There could be as many as ten KPIs governing issues such as punctuality, efficiency, perhaps tidiness of paperwork or dress. If you have hired a salesperson, you need to give them very clear, defined targets, and they will thank you for it. Half of an employee's salary could be performance-based against those KPIs. By setting out these criteria right from the start, you make sure there will be no confusion later.

Here is an example of a key performance indicator I would use to measure the success of a salesperson. Their salary would be made up of a basic wage, plus commission based on this formula: I would expect 100 enquiries to turn into 40 appointments – a ratio of 10:4; those 40 appointments must lead to 15 sales – a ratio of 4:1.5; to qualify for a bonus, they must hit those ratios over the course of a month.

In the corporate playground there are very similar rules to those set at school, where, if a teacher was strict, you knew where you stood. If your homework was late you knew there would be a problem. It is the same with staff. If they know they can get away with it, they will. If someone is late there has to be a reprimand of some sort because, if there isn't, that person will be late again and again. If your sales team don't hit their targets, you need to let them know you are not happy.

To inspect what you expect is important. If you expect people to be punctual, make sure you notice when they are late. Keeping people on their toes is no bad thing. It is very easy for complacency to set in. You get this in large businesses where the level of motivation slides and people coast from day to day. They keep their heads down and collect their salary, which is marvellous for them but not for you or your business. When you keep people on their toes, they know that, in return for their salary, they are expected to be productive.

I describe it to people like this. The money I am paying them is in exchange for their time and expertise. I am investing in them and I expect them to earn it with their skill and time. If employees are frequently sick or absent I often ask them, 'Would you like me to drop your salary by 25 per cent because I am only getting three-quarters of the time I have paid for?' They bluster, 'That's absolutely ridiculous, you can't do that!' But it makes them think.

Do not allow your staff to use business time for personal matters. Calls from the boyfriend, sending personal emails and using your stamps for their private letters is not acceptable. I purchase 37.5 hours a week from my staff and, during that period, their time belongs to me. If I am hiring an outside consultant to work for me for three hours a week, they come in and work for three hours. They do not stop after an hour and make a personal phone call, check their emails and nip down to the post office to renew their car tax. For those three hours, they are working for me, and that is precisely what I am paying them for. It is exactly the same thing with your staff.

A lot of people take work for granted. They feel it is their right to have the job. It takes a shift in thinking for people to realise that it is a privilege to be employed and that they will actually enjoy their working day far more if they put more into it. It is wonderful when you meet an employee who says, 'I think of this as my own company. I don't feel as though I'm spending the company's money, it's as if I'm spending my own. I have a pride in my work and I want to do the very best.' I would much rather have them than someone who says, 'I won't send that email until Monday because no one'll notice.'

The self-motivated employee realises that it will be noticed and it reflects badly on the company. They are the people who should be sacking their boss because, if you can't motivate yourself when you are working for someone else, there is no way you will ever be self-motivated when you are the boss. It is a recipe for disaster. It is not going to be an easy life working for yourself – it will be tougher – but, believe me, the rewards will be bigger. I am not a great people manager. I am better than I was and it is definitely a skill that can be learned.

When your first employee leaves it is tragic. Later on, as you become more experienced, you realise that, when a member of staff leaves, it is probably for the best. It is better for them to get out now, rather than stay on when they no longer want to be there. If it is not working out for them, it isn't working for you and if you are not happy, believe me, they are not happy being there either.

EXIT STRATEGY

If sacking your boss has been a success, you may have ended up with lots of staff. That is when many entrepreneurs wonder why they ever started a business in the first place.

The whole point of starting a business is freedom, not to give you headaches about things you absolutely hate and despise. One ghastly thought you may have to face up to in the future is this: Are the skills that allowed me to start this business enough to take it to the next level? Do I have what it takes to run a business with fifty staff as well as I did with just five?

Quite often this is the moment when the entrepreneur has to back down, so what is your exit strategy? How do you walk away from the business you gave birth to and nurtured from that momentous day when you sacked your boss? Do you sell your company? Do you step down from the day-to-day operation and become the chair while a managing director looks after the business? Do you exit completely or should you be the sole or major shareholder and let other people run it? I believe that when this happens something in the company dies.

 Would Dyson still be Dyson without James Dyson? Would Virgin really be Virgin without Richard Branson? Stelios has been brought back into easyJet to give it back its flair.

When a hired managing director is brought in, the business loses its spark as well as the credible belief in the future provided by an entrepreneur. Would Dyson still be Dyson without James Dyson? Would

Virgin really be Virgin without Richard Branson? To illustrate the point, Stelios has been brought back into easyJet to give it back its flair. If I were a business coach of an entrepreneur facing that dilemma, I would ask, 'Why did you start this business in the first place?' That way you will find out exactly what was the original motivation for sacking the boss. I would then ask, 'What did you love about the business right at the start and how do we get that back?'

When you are a business owner you often end up doing things you don't like. You don't set out to do them but you carry on doing them so you forget why you went into business in the first place. It could be that one of the reasons you decided to go it alone was to take more holidays. Fine, take more holidays, then. Surely there is someone on the staff who is just itching to have more responsibility. Usually, problems are caused by a lack of delegation. I now find that, if I go away for several weeks, I do phone the office but I don't have to. In fact, I phone with an expectant kind of voice, secretly hoping there will be some terrible disaster for me to tackle! I actually feel as if I am being slightly irritating by asking if everything is all right.

A few months before writing this, I started to feel very unloved and I began to realise that my business doesn't actually need me any more. That is probably the point at which the entrepreneur says, 'What's next? What else can I do?'

SO WHAT ARE YOU WAITING FOR?

You have decided to join the Sack Your Boss Revolution and now is the time to act. The time has come to put all the practical advice I have given you based on my own experience into action. I have put together an action plan made up of six broad steps. You can adapt this to suit your particular needs and your business.

ACTION PLAN

1. **Decide what your new business is going to be.** Set out a vision of your new venture, but be prepared for it to change as your business grows and expands. If, for example, you want to manufacture greetings cards, you might find that people keep asking you to make gift tags instead. At that stage, you might discover that there is a better market in another side of the business, so be prepared for it to take on a life of its own and evolve in ways you had not anticipated.

2. **Set your goals.** You need to write out two sets of goals. The first is what you want to achieve personally. This could be financial independence, perhaps to achieve a better work–life balance or maybe spend more time with your family. The second is what you want the business to achieve. Do you want to end up with a business that is completely self-sufficient, or do you want it to be you and one other person?

3. **Set out six steps to getting there.** By working backwards, set out six steps to achieving those goals. If self-sufficiency is the goal and there are six steps to getting there, Step Six would be hiring a manager to run the business and employing a number of department heads. To reach that goal, Step One might be to get a hundred customers so you can employ the first member of staff.

4. **Work out a timescale for each step.** Allocate a timescale for each step, otherwise you can drift for months putting off each one. You might want to set a goal of getting a hundred customers within twelve months. To get those hundred customers you need to have business cards printed. The timescale on that might be one week. Make sure the steps are prioritised and in a logical order.

5. **Plan your marketing strategy.** You need to work out how much you are going to charge. How are you going to get your customers and, once you have them, how are you going to delight those clients? They must be so pleased with your service and product that they keep coming back and will refer other customers to you.

6. **Start at number one!**

Now you have read the book and have left your job or are about to, why not look again at your wheel of business success. I have printed the wheel again below, so you can fill it in and see how confident you now feel in each area. Each month or so, have another look at it and note how you are progressing in the various areas that will make you a business success. The idea is to get your inner wheel as near to a perfect circle as possible.

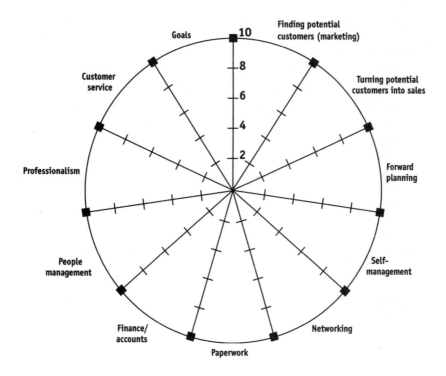

TELL ME HOW YOU SACKED YOUR BOSS

Now that you have travelled my journey with me and found out about the ups and downs of starting your own business through my experiences, I wish you the very best in your successful new venture. When you are in charge of your own business venture, why not write to me and tell me how you sacked your boss, hired yourself and never looked back? I want to hear from everyone who has used this book as a step on the road to running their own business.

Tell me how you sacked your boss, how you started the business, how it grew, how your life has changed because you got rid of your boss and became your own employer.

Contact me at jonathan@iwanttosackmyboss.com.

BIBLIOGRAPHY

Abraham, Jay *Getting Everything You Can Out of All You've Got: 21 Ways You can Out-think, Out-perform and Out-earn the Competition*. Piatkus.

Alden, Chris *The Guardian Media Directory 2006*. Guardian Books.

Barlin, Paul *The Freelance Photographers' Market Handbook*. BFP Books.

Berman Fortgang, Laura *Take Yourself to the Top*. Thorsons.

Brown, Mick *Richard Branson: The Authorised Biography*. Headline.

Gerber, Michael *The E-Myth Revisited*. HarperBusiness, US.

Maltz, Maxwell *The New Psycho-Cybernetics: The Original Science of Self-Improvement and Success that Has Changed the Lives of 30 Million People*. Souvenir Press.

PIMS directories www.pims.co.uk – 020 7562 6550

Robbins, Tony *Awaken The Giant Within*. Simon & Schuster.

Tracy, Brian *Eat That Frog*. Hodder & Stoughton.

Turner, Barry *The Writer's Handbook*. Macmillan.

Willings Press Guide www.willingspress.com

Writers' & Artists' Yearbook. London: A & C Black.